MEMORY OF ELSEWHERE

Memory of Elsewhere

RONA MURRAY

Sono
Nis
Press

VICTORIA B.C. CANADA

CANADIAN CATALOGUING IN PUBLICATION DATA

Murray, Rona, 1924-
  Memory of elsewhere

  ISBN 1-55039-100-3

  1. Near-death experiences. 2. Murray, Rona, 1924. I. Title.
PS8526.U762Z53 2000   133.9'01'3   C00-910324-4
PR9199.3.M83Z466 2000

Sono Nis Press gratefully acknowledges the support of the Canada Council for the Arts and of the Province of British Columbia, through the British Columbia Arts Council.

Cover illustration: "Arch V," by Heather Keenan
Cover and interior design by Jim Brennan

Patricia Young's poem "Three Days Before Christmas," from *What I Remember from My Time on Earth*, copyright © Patricia Young, 1997, is reprinted by permission of House of Anansi Press Limited.

Some of the material in the chapter "Possibility" previously appeared in *Western Living*, October 1994.

Published by
SONO NIS PRESS
PO Box 5550, Stn. B
Victoria, BC V8R 6S4
tel: (250) 598-7807
sono.nis@islandnet.com
http://www.islandnet.com/sononis/

Printed and bound in Canada by Friesens

For Pat, I hope you enjoy this. With love from Joan.

This book is dedicated to all
who love and protect the earth

OTHER BOOKS BY RONA MURRAY

Poetry:

The Enchanted Adder, 1965
The Power of the Dog, 1968
Ootischenie, 1974
Selected Poems, 1974
Journey, 1981
Adam and Eve in Middle Age, 1984
The Lost Garden (chapbook), 1993

Fiction:

The Indigo Dress and Other Stories, 1986

Memoir/Travel:

Journey Back to Peshawar, 1993

Anthologies (ed.):
The Art of Earth, 1979
Threshold, 1998

ACKNOWLEDGEMENTS

I should particularly like to thank my editor Barbara Colebrook Peace for her painstaking work and encouragement and also Susan Gibson for reading this manuscript enthusiastically and making several suggestions, most of which I have employed. Her husband, Dr. Allan D. Stone, checked over my sketchy knowledge of quantum mechanics and gently added workable information. My publisher, Diane Morriss, let me know from the start she would publish this book and that it was worth writing. Her copy editor Dawn Loewen, a generous and rigorous taskmaster, corrected some doubtful information and hunted up books containing pertinent knowledge. Theodore Haimberger has always been available to help with his knowledge of computers and, with extraordinary generosity, gave me a new laptop so I could work in my "little house," overlooking the sea and away from interruptions. Dorothy Cauldwell kindly sent me the information on "whole cloth," and Aaron Johannes invited me to his wedding where I read one of the Blessings referred to in the text.

Milton Carmen instantly picked up enthusiastically on my faint suggestion that perhaps I could extend an original essay into a worthwhile book and pointed out ways in which I could do so. Finally, I have a husband who wishes he could lock me up, as Colette untruthfully claimed her husband locked her up, in order to force me to write, so I should thank him too. He is the most patient of men.

*C*ONTENTS

ACCIDENT

❦

IT WAS NEAR THE END OF JANUARY, 1994, and a breathtakingly clear day after a month of rain.

I was alone on my way to buy groceries and was driving up a slight incline which passes through a gravel pit, the largest on the west coast of North America, close to where I live. I was used to the pit with its ungainly machines, replicas of prehistoric creatures, moving mountains of earth and no longer noticed them. The sea to my right glittered under a winter sun breaking through clouds and warming the earth into a lovely, almost spring day. I felt exceptionally lighthearted with a sense of being lifted up out of a vague, grey indifference. This was the southern tip of Vancouver Island, exquisite in its natural beauty but often subject to dull raining winters. Now it was so unexpectedly warm that I longed to get back and see if the ground was dry enough to do some gardening. I wanted to thrust a spade into the heavy clay soil and turn it over, to examine snowdrops breaking cover and hellebores, just blooming or with tight, dark mauve buds.

I have no memory of a car approaching. It was driven, I was told later, by a man with a sympathetic name, Mr. Peacock, who apparently had a history of small heart attacks or seizures. I must have seen the car since the police later said I turned the wheel in an attempt to avoid it when the driver blacked out, pulled his wheel round, and drove straight into my driver's door, pushing the car about twenty feet into rough grassland and a ditch.

In the hospital, the only moment of consciousness during the accident I could recall was a flash in which there was no surprise or pain: a dream in which people were trying to get me out of a car. Later I was told it took close to an hour to extricate me, and when I saw photographs of my almost-new white Cavalier, it seemed astonishing I was alive at all. At the time my body was rushed to hospital, X-rayed and CAT-scanned; my husband, who had been phoned, watched nurses and doctors moving me from stretcher to machine and was appalled by the pain I was in. For me, it's all gone. I do remember a moment in which a doctor (probably an intern) was carefully stitching my forehead and was anxious about glass fragments. He did a fine job and put in over a hundred stitches in a very small space. I felt nothing. When I was fully conscious, I found cuts and embedded glass in my hands, an excruciatingly painful left side to my body but no broken bones, and what turned out to be a ruptured spleen but not, as doctors feared, a ruptured aorta.

My glasses, found fifty yards down the road, were scratched but not broken. My watch still worked: it had continued patiently to record, second by second, my life in the process of dribbling away.

I'd been physically active, fairly quick in my movements, an enthusiastic hiker, gardener, swimmer, but now found myself tied to a bed by tubes: four attached to a vein in my neck and a catheter. Later there would be another up my nose. Apparently I appeared reasonably alert to visitors; some stared intently into my eyes, others told me indecipherable jokes and sometimes fascinating stories. A tall, thin, slightly mad German filmmaker found me the perfect audience for a movie he was planning to make: "Now you know that little building down by the water where the golfers go? They go for lunch if they choose to avoid their club. Expensive . . . drinks . . . you know. Well, God is running a short-order grill in that building for those bizarre people in plus fours and English golfing caps. Those people don't understand God, an Italian with crazy language, hairy arms, and secret purposes. . . ." The script was more real than I was. I listened in a delicious dream, not expected to respond or comment.

Cards arrived, flowers, fruit, books, homemade soups brought by people who knew hospital food—and all I had to do was lie there, wrapped in gratitude for having been given a secret gift of the kind one observes sideways, in silence, not daring to examine too closely in case it disappears as a dream disappears when the sleeper is pulled roughly back by a ringing bell. For a long time I didn't tell anyone about this gift, not because I thought the telling would bore people or that I would be pitied for having become unbalanced by the blow to my head, but because I was afraid of destroying a revelation which would drop away in tatters if I exposed it to the light. Later, I still did not want to talk about it; it seemed too private.

One of those tubes in my neck contained morphine I was to administer to myself and the nurses were upset I didn't use it. They told me I wouldn't become addicted. It hadn't occurred to me I might. I didn't need it. I was entirely happy except when I had to move and found the pain intense. It didn't bother me at all that I was about to have some kind of operation or that my stomach was becoming extended as if the blood and fluid being dripped into me were forming a lake in my belly at about a seven months' pregnancy level. I did wonder briefly why I hadn't been asked if I wanted transfusions. When a social worker came in and told me on no account to settle compensation for at least a year, I was surprised, not having considered anything of the kind. Pushed to think about it, I didn't feel justified in demanding anything; I'd been through an astonishingly positive experience, been given the greatest compensation possible. I mentioned this indifference to a friend who became concerned and told me not to be an idiot, to think of my children's needs.

When I wasn't in a delicious dream, recalling a floating bliss which was more real to me than possibly anything else in my life had been, I read fiction but almost at once forgot not only the contents and feel of the book but also the title and author. My short-term memory had been selectively wiped out. As it happened, I also had an ear infection and couldn't hear the conversation going on in the ward. This was a blessing because I was able to exist in my dream state without having to take part in the general talk around me. When the infection cleared up, I realized how fortunate I'd been. The ward held four women, all of us middle-aged or aging, and an almost unceasing chatter around ailments, operations, and doctors.

The last thing I wanted to do was to listen or be part of it.

Mr. Peacock and I had been alone on a fairly long stretch of excellent road. One second sooner or later, the major part of the damage would have been avoided; perhaps the accident would have been avoided entirely. Later this gave me much to think about. I wondered if some kind of destiny was at work here, if my essential self, grown complacent and without growth, hadn't needed a kick forward. But pragmatically this appeared absurd. With millions of people, a teeming mass of busy ants, on this planet, let alone whatever may be happening on other planets, how could each one be given individual attention, a destiny to follow, possibly a tutelary deity or medieval angel to make sure a particular course is completed? This possibility was more strongly in my head after the accident than it is today; I've tended to lapse back into a mundane world. Even so, it's not entirely dismissed. I think of a novel which was still popular when I was in my teens, Thornton Wilder's *The Bridge of San Luis Rey*, written in 1927, which had posed as its central conundrum why particular people had been on a bridge when it collapsed. Of course, this is an age-old question and today, with unremitting violence and casual death on constant display, we can hardly be naive enough to ask it. Even so, most of us still wish for some kind of explanation for suffering and inexplicable death, or at least some interest on the part of an unknown outside force. Wilder appears to sidestep the issue, but he doesn't actually, because outside forces, indifferent or diligent, are still there: "Some say . . . to the gods we are like the flies that the boys kill on a summer day, and some say, on the contrary, that the very sparrows do not lose a feather that has not been brushed away by the finger of God."

Gurkhas, once a part of my world since as a child I lived in a military cantonment in India, are fatalistic: the reason no doubt for their renowned courage. If they do not die under heavy fire, they are modest, surprised by praise and medals, saying, "It was not written on my forehead," a presumption some metaphorical finger has written the date of a final encounter.

During the accident, my "I", knowledge of self, was removed from the car and appeared to be a considerable distance above it. Place was not a consideration and is only mentioned because that "I", an ecstatic, "knowing" duplicate of this unknowing, everyday I, had a swift, non-detailed overview of earth. It had no reference to the physical me in an accident but was, I knew, the real me. I don't know if this "I" was attached to a body of some kind—it wasn't important. I do know it experienced limitless freedom, energy, enthusiasm, purpose, self-confidence, and joy. In everyday consciousness these attributes exist, if at all, to a degree; in that state, there was no space for doubt.

This experience may be what some enthusiastically charismatic Christians call spiritual orgasm and Hindus refer to as bliss: both more comprehensive terms than my lame account. Dostoevsky's rapt description of epilepsy, "the falling sickness," labelled by many cultures as the holy malady, is far better. In a recent publication, *Phantoms of the Brain*, neuroscientist V. S. Ramachandran discusses the "God lobe," a part of the temporal lobes, which he claims produces this mystical experience during an epileptic seizure. He considers the possibility that this area of the brain produces these ecstatic feelings either for evolutionary value or for the deliberate construction of a venue leading to our communication with another reality.

In an essay on Dostoevsky, Thomas Mann discusses his

attacks and their psychological effects:

> Two symptoms . . . are of inner enlightenment,
> of harmony, of highest ecstasy, preceding by
> a few moments the spasm that begins with an
> inarticulate, no longer human scream—and the
> state of horrible depression and deep grief, of
> spiritual ruin and desolation, that follows it.

Mann is interested in the desolation and guilt that follow an attack, but let's look again at the first step: the inner enlightenment, harmony, ecstasy. He continues: "Dostoevsky describes it as a rapture so strong and sweet 'that one is ready to exchange ten years of life or even life itself for the bliss of these few seconds.'"

That's the bliss I'm talking about. For me, it was not followed by guilt or remorse but lingered as perfume might—not to be recreated, but to be savoured as long as possible.

During the experience, the "I" was completely in the present; it wasn't looking to the past or future, although it had a sense it was on its way to, or could be going to, a known place. It was alone but in no way lonely, and it was certain of two things. The first was that there's no difference between life and death— all is one. A bank of fog lies between two coasts, that's all, and the sun shines on both coasts equally, even if to one the other appears obscured by heavy fog. The other truth was that it didn't matter in the least if I lived or died, to me, or, ultimately, anyone else. Occasionally now I feel as if I have to push away my preconceptions in an almost physical way if I want to understand this.

Years ago, before my own experience, a friend, Elizabeth, told me briefly she had been in a nearly fatal accident. She probably told me because she was scarred from burns, particularly down one arm, and perhaps wanted me to know the cause. She spoke casually, didn't go into detail, so all I know is that she was beside a gasoline pump, sitting in her car, when fire exploded, engulfing her. Badly burned, she spent months in hospital. She said that during the accident she was not aware of pain and knew it didn't matter if she lived or died because there was no difference between the two. At the time she told me, this lack of difference made little sense; I couldn't comprehend what she was talking about. But she wasn't prepared to go on—it was as if she had nothing more to add or didn't want to talk about it. It was just something she knew but found difficult to discuss. There was no question of her telling me of this experience, as I sometimes feel others have on similar topics, to impress me with her superior spirituality, and we did not return to the topic.

Recently on a meditation retreat I met another woman, Jan, who, days after I'd told my story, said she'd had the same experience years before when she was bleeding to death during a spontaneous abortion. She'd never forgotten her miraculous taste of bliss, but had told no one about it. For a long time she'd puzzled privately over what had occurred and had finally arrived at the conclusion that endorphins, released as natural painkillers, may have given her this astonishing high accompanied with more or less the same kinds of knowledge I gained. By the time I met her, she'd decided the whole episode

Rona Murray

had a physical basis only, but added that if what we regard as the supreme creative power (electrical force, Jehovah, Brahma, God, Allah) is actually a part of us, is us, that part would have known to release a flood of well-being into its own living tissue in its need. I don't think she quite believed this, but it was the nearest she could come to an acceptable explanation.

I've noticed people are hesitant about mentioning this kind of experience, I think out of embarrassment. Nobody wants to be considered "odd" or, in documented cases, crazy. Or perhaps the event seems so private that it becomes something of a personal secret. I still don't really want to discuss it orally—it is easier to write about it. As a result of this reticence, one may draw the conclusion that the experience is far more common than we suppose. A few days ago I was talking to a friend I had not seen for some time, and she asked me what I was doing. I told her I was trying to write a book with a publisher's deadline and was having some difficulty. She asked me what my manuscript was based on, and with hesitation I gave her the briefest idea.

She said, "Oh, yes, I know."

"What do you mean?"

"It happened to me when Robin was born. I didn't have drugs and thought it must have been a reaction to the pain, which was intense. It was floating bliss."

"Do you remember exactly?"

"Of course. It was *conscious* separation. I was floating above the bed with the doctor at the end of it and Roger in the middle. There was blood. I knew such bliss and then terror that if I didn't get back I would drift divinely out of the white window—pulled backwards, as if I was hauling on a rope which was pulling the other way. It took a supreme act of will to get back into my body. Jung has written about the same kind of thing. In *Memories, Dreams, Reflections*."

As soon as I could, I pulled a battered copy of Jung's memoir out of a bookshelf. I had read it years before, an account filled with night dreams and day visions, but had forgotten this near-death telling:

> At the beginning of 1944 I broke my foot, and this misadventure was followed by a heart attack. In a state of unconsciousness I experienced deliriums and visions which must have begun when I hung on the edge of death and was being given oxygen and camphor injections. The images were so tremendous that I myself concluded that I was close to death. My nurse afterward told me, "It was as if you were surrounded by a bright glow." That was a phenomenon she had sometimes observed in the dying, she added. I had reached the outermost limit, and do not know whether I was in a dream or an ecstasy. . . .
>
> It seemed to me that I was high up in space. Far below I saw the globe of the earth, bathed in a gloriously blue light. . . . I knew I was on the point of departing from the earth. [After his discovery, described in detail, that he was the sum of all he had ever experienced or done and that there was no longer anything he

truth. An Indian woodcut illustrates Kali standing between Man and Brahma, both of whom hold their arms above their heads. Each has only one hand. Brahma is saying, "You are not perfect? Well, why worry, I am not perfect either." They reflect each other, are one and the same, and are not complete, are evolving. The sacred Hindu Vedas state: "The wise man's God is his inner self." Mystics, Christian and otherwise, bend their energies attempting to achieve unity with, indivisibility from, what we call God. They seek non-duality, no longer this/that; me/you; or life/death.

I had read and heard all this, had meditated in an undisciplined way, but had failed to experience any of it in a real sense. Possibly, however, I did begin to approach a different reality (and deny it at once by placing the knowledge in time) when Mr. Peacock had a blackout and ran into me going through a gravel pit in Metchosin on Vancouver Island.

My experience may be considered only a partial breakthrough by those who have had other significations. I had no sense of oneness with a deity as in the mystics' records, but I also had no sense of separateness, so perhaps I was "at one" without thinking about it. I did not have to think about it. The deep "I" part of me already knew this was its reality. A deity didn't come into it, was not part of the experience, not desired or necessary. Instead, while it lasted, I was wholly consciousness, nested in love, and exactly where I belonged.

This doesn't mean that I've grasped what happened, that it has radically changed my exterior life; I think it could have done that, but didn't. Nor does it mean I can make the experience real for others. I believe my task, if only for my own unfolding, is to remember and recall and be grateful. The joy and confidence embedded in the knowledge *that it is all all right* (everything, even including what appalls us) cannot be denied. The real me was, for that moment or for those hours, awake from a transient dream. The knowledge did not deny the horrendous acts which take place in that dream or the existence of depravation, evil, excruciating pain, but acknowledged these would not occur if we were truly awake. We would know we are maiming and killing and hurting ourselves or, as the Doukhobors say, the Christ within each of us.

❈

This suggestion of a cosmic oneness, a great stillness at the heart of being, embodying everything we know (so insignificantly little) and don't know, takes a mental earthquake shift because we've been imprinted with inner and outer, you and me, this and that, and the reality of diversity and multiples. We have been trained to think in terms of an inscrutable, all-powerful God contrasted with a somewhat pitiable us. However, not only mystics and metaphysicians explore non-duality. It's the basis of the quantum theory of physics. Some scientists suggest the universe is a single electrical construct. Modern physicists talk about the earth and all it contains as a living organism, part of a living universe. Biologist Lewis Thomas in *The Lives of a Cell* hypothesizes that all earth matter started as a single cell and we, along with everything else, evolved from that cell, bound together, a part of all that exists and of each other:

> The uniformity of the earth's life, more astonishing than its diversity, is accountable by the

high probability that we derived, originally, from some single cell, fertilized in a bolt of lightning as the earth cooled. It is from the progeny of this parent cell that we take our looks; we still share genes around, and the enzymes of grasses to those of whales is a family resemblance.

One can more easily think of the universe as a spider's web with each twist linking the whole.

There's comfort in this theory because there you are in your right place: a tiny, indispensable fragment—not to be judged by human judgement—with a position and purpose in the web of being, no matter what you have done in your pain and ignorance.

To return to the second thing the "I" knew: it didn't matter in the least, to itself or others, if the usual I lived or died. In the known dimension, if death were imminent, any one of us would think of family left behind and possibly in need of support, commitments unfulfilled, careers and tasks which we believe to be important abandoned. But out of time, the "I" knew perfectly well that without the usual me around everything would take care of itself, within the bounds of probability, and that what appears materially important to us is not. This, as far as I recall—I wasn't thinking consciously, I simply knew—included events which we would consider earth-shattering.

Connected with my being on metaphysical tiptoe, about to be off to a known destination, I knew the freedom which comes from the release of all commitments. Promises given, events experienced during our tiny experiment in unknowing hold no significance. One's reality is so altered, old pledges are no longer valid. Thinking about this later, I remembered the publicly sworn oaths made by Oliver Lodge and Conan Doyle, ardent spiritualists, that the one who died first would contact the other, presumably through a medium (now known as a channeller). Nothing happened. No message was given, either one to the other or to the world at large. Perhaps each took off in a swoosh of joy.

Like others, and I think this is far from unusual, I have had the odd unexpected visitation although I disclaim having any psychic ability—at least more than anyone else. One small episode was so direct, with such undeniable detail, that I can't easily dismiss it. Soon after my second marriage, long before the car accident, my father-in-law was ill and my husband went to him, arriving just after his death. I remained in our house in a remote area of British Columbia with our German shepherd, a rather ferocious dog which was nevertheless terrified by a storm of sheet and forked lightning with wind that flattened fully grown aspen trees parallel with the earth. I sat restlessly at the dining room table trying to edit some poems when I was aware of an image in front of me. Not real and not imaginary, something in between, there was my father-in-law, a man I did not know well and was not thinking about. I didn't know he had actually died close to that moment. He was dressed for a journey in a dark overcoat, a hat and gloves, and was carrying a briefcase. He didn't use words but let me know he was pleased that his son (he'd apparently been concerned about him) had a new companion and he himself was delighted to be off, sessions of cruel headaches and a monotonous life over with. I'd never seen him with the energy and joy this figure demonstrated nor dressed so formally in clothes which gave their own message.

Years before, when my children were small and I was exhausted, I lay one afternoon, curtains closed, on my back on the bed and, wide awake, "knew" a huge white figure, half angel, half bird, perched without weight on my diaphragm, metaphorically marking that space; its wings were so enormous, they stretched through the ceiling and high into the air above the roof. No fear attached itself to this peculiar vision; it seemed as if I were being given a message: something special I had to do or learn. I hope, if this was not purely imaginary, which of course it may have been, the message was not a summons to action of some kind as I've done nothing spectacular in my life. In my heart I'm an activist in a social sense but am also, unless pushed externally, lazy, shy, and lacking in self-confidence, so take the easier place by the sidelines.

We all, or at least most of us, hesitate before acknowledging visitations of this kind, chiefly out of embarrassment. We are afraid of what others may think, possibly because we live in a technological, materialist age. Past literature, however, is rampant with angelic figures, visitations, magic, and dreams. That world may be just as close to the truth as ours is. At the time, I wrote a poem; the one or two people who read it took it as relating to sexual love, not at all its intent. It was discarded so thoroughly, I've had to hunt through ancient papers to find it; even so, it illustrates what I felt at the time. I called it "Visitation":

The narrow room could not contain

that fierce angel; flaming pinions
seraphated through the non-confining
lath and plaster frailties of man.

He burned his brand below my heart;
burned not with hand or iron, but there
the cipher grew, a confirmation
of that angelic act. Alien, tender,
close, unpossessed, quivering splendour
shone into the dark. No refutation
may deny the seal with which he placed
his mark.

My experience during the car accident was not in its details
Christian: there was no tunnel, no white light, no soft music,
no meeting with "loved ones" (a term I dislike as too facile, not
necessarily true), or with Jesus. I was not given the choice,
which appears to be fairly common, to return to earth or to go
on somewhere else (the "known" destination?); I simply found
myself in a hospital bed. More may have occurred than I
remembered because I was not in the least surprised at where I
was. A week or so later, the surgeon who removed my battered
spleen was dramatic when he learned I smoked, angrily pointing
out I'd had a "zero", had been pulled back, and in gratitude
should not do anything so foolish. I have no memory of being
pulled back, willing or unwilling, unlike many, but not all, of
those who have encountered much the same thing. In many
cases, of course, the details differ, but from all I have read and
heard, the actual experience in its comprehension of harmony

and bliss has been the same, never with doubt that it was illusory.

It doesn't end there, of course. What kinds of near-death episodes have been survived by Buddhists, Hindus, Moslems, Jews? People of these faiths and/or traditions have obviously come close to dying and have lived to recall and bear witness to it. Their literature is rich in transcendental reality but generally not linked to near-death. Some mention other ecstatic approaches—drugs, sex, dance (whirling dervishes)—which hope to, or do, arrive at the same destination. When I tried to describe, in a euphoric state, my own reality to a Buddhist, he pointed out I had reached a plateau for which meditators strive and which individuals may reach without killing, or nearly killing, themselves. This was a joke rather than a suggestion the accident was karmic, engendered by the "I" that knows.

There are other questions. Having been granted this revelation, would I and others who have also experienced it be afraid if we were faced with sudden death? If we were in front of a firing squad, a romantic and unlikely possibility? If a violent madman broke into the house with a knife or gun—not quite so unlikely—would we shrink back in terror? What about an imminent plane crash? I don't know. I do know at times I've longed to return to the place I was in, and I do know others have felt the same way.

Walt Whitman, the great American transcendentalist with his "robust soul," who knew well the delight and anguish our small love affair with material existence entails, lived close to violent death as a medical orderly during the American Civil War. He wrote in *Leaves of Grass*:

Has anyone supposed it lucky to be born?
I hasten to inform him or her it is just as lucky to die, and
    I know it.

Whitman, according to Richard Bucke, a Canadian doctor who wrote *Cosmic Consciousness*, had experienced something similar to my kind of explosive certainty; others are legion. Blake. Bucke himself. They didn't need to be on the verge of death to know a different reality. When I reread *Leaves of Grass*, as I've done recently, I kept thinking, yes, that's what it was like. Whitman expressed what I knew briefly and although the revelation may not have changed me into a more tolerant, less self-indulgent, more wise and loving person, I did experience it and it has forced me to stand back; to observe, weigh, and consider situations and behaviours more than I did previously. I appear to be distanced in some way, and concerns which were once important—a need for success and acknowledgement, for example—are no longer so.

One way of regarding life is that we follow a continuum. As far as we know, Whitman did not need an extraordinary experience to push him along a path he was already treading. He had an abiding confidence in what he was doing: writing, self-publishing, rewriting, and again self-publishing his poems. He knew he had something important to communicate. He had no need for other people's opinions. A steady travelling of our universal journey is illustrated by an anecdote recounted by Charles Olsen, the Black Mountain poet, in 1963. It was not original with him but came, he said, from an Arabic source: from the day we start our journey, our angel also starts towards us and when we meet we combine and walk as one in the direction from which the angel came. If we avoid this meeting, we are incomplete and have to repeat the journey until we have learned what we have to learn and can go forward. We are not radically changed but are more ourselves. The meeting does not have to be painful, or may be; it does not have to catapult us into wisdom or understanding, but it must be significant. At the time I heard the story, I wrote this poem:

It was then that I met my angel;
we did not turn aside, he and I,
but confronted each other, hostile
and proud in our walking,
and it seemed a stillness was born
as we stood naked waiting
to combine form with form.

O it was not easy, and even after
(foot braced to foot, thigh to thigh)
we pierced each other's bone
no words may tell the pain.

It was a long time, that curious
mating, and I not prepared to pound
muscle and mind and flesh
into fragments demanded
by this tall stranger,
he who had been approaching the place
of meeting since that day I lay
rejected by the womb in which
my frame was created.

Each cell must break, he said;
we will then return the way I have come.
His feet marked the dust,
his hand the breast,
his wings drove submission.

We turned and walked the edge of creation;
no abyss nor mountain could alter
the road we had taken.

The jewel (stone) of the Tibetan mantra, the journey, the
experience and metaphor of the angel, come together in an
extract from an essay by Marie-Luise von Franz writing on Jung's
speculations:

> The alchemical stone (the *lapis*) symbol-
> izes something that can never be lost or
> dissolved, something eternal that some alche-
> mists compared to the mystical experience of
> God within one's own soul. It usually takes pro-
> longed suffering to burn away all the
> superfluous psychic elements concealing the
> stone. But some profound inner experience of
> the Self does occur to most people at least once
> in a lifetime. From the psychological stand-
> point, a genuinely religious attitude consists
> of an effort to discover this unique experience,
> and gradually to keep in tune with it (it is rel-
> evant that a stone is itself something

permanent), so that the Self becomes an inner partner toward whom one's attention is continually turned.

❦

It's over four years since I had the car accident, and there are far worse accidents with probably more pain but, as Plato said, the unexamined life is not worth living, so I need to consider this event, to "keep in tune" with it, and mine from it any understanding or knowledge that I can.

To me, as to others, it has always seemed extraordinary we should be on a globe spinning through space without having the faintest idea whether we are here by accident or design. If by design, why? If by accident, how unlikely. We know little more now than King Edwin and his counsellors did in the seventh century when they decided to adopt Christianity because, as one old man said in a famous passage from Bede's *Anglo-Saxon Chronicle*, man's life is like the flight of a sparrow in wintertime through a room where a fire is lighted, a table laid, and men are eating and drinking, filled with good food and joy. The bird comes in at one door and for a moment is safe from the wintry storm, but almost immediately vanishes out through another into the darkness from which it had emerged: "So this life of man appears for a short space, but of what went before or what is to follow we are utterly ignorant." He ends by concluding that this new religion is as good as any other and might comfort man, so why not adopt it? A pragmatic fellow.

At times we have a perception that the answer is just around the corner. Occasionally I've had an overwhelming conviction, which may be common, that the era is approaching when everything will be revealed, the mystery finished with, as if we are standing on the edge of a continent filled with promise. Not long ago a theory emerged that life was seeded on the earth—seeded like grass—and whoever (some kind of outer space intelligence?) had cast the seed had done so as an experiment, then stood back to see what would happen, ready to acknowledge its role at the appropriate time. According to this theory that time may be approaching, because we are now able to, and no doubt eventually will, disrupt the solar system (galaxy?) with our knowledge of atomic conflagration. We can no longer be left alone to play such dangerous games. A poetic theory; one among many.

Perhaps it's this expectation—the gates will be opened—that persuades those who join fundamentalist religions and outrageously demanding sects to do so. And possibly it's the same kind of hunger that persuades people who have had "near-death" or "out-of-body" experiences that some form of consciousness continues after death and that living on this earth in this particular life is a temporary exile. The mind plays a multitude of tricks on us, we create our own reality, so we should well hesitate to claim that any intimation of the "other" (which is inevitably outside the possibility of proof) is actual. However, since we are all ignorant, any glimmer is at least worthy of consideration.

I recognize I have no doubt always responded to the life of the senses. Now having been given this glimpse of another reality, I've been left with a still greater need to look, touch, listen, inhale, and examine the physical world, not with desperation but with urgency, not exactly with reverence but certainly with desire. I desire to know so much more of the actual than I've given time to in the past. This earth has become infinitely precious. I want to handle the loam when I'm gardening, remark its dark shine when a spade first tilts it open, take time to consider the conversion of waste material into rich earth by micro-organisms, observe bees going from one circle of stamens to another while packing pollen into their back pockets, hear the variations in their cordial humming; I desire to look inside flowers, examine their exact patterns of colour, their sexual organs, and at night stare into the sky, watch the moon, stars, planets and find out more about their origins, their possibilities. I persuaded my husband to give me a microscope for Christmas but I haven't used it. I bought a telescope and have barely attempted to focus it. In love, we are impetuous to know everything about the beloved, but finally we seldom take the time truthfully to know that beloved. In this case, the beloved is the earth, and we are aware, as lovers are, even if subconsciously, that all its extraordinary richness may be lost to us at any moment, and we may never have the chance to taste its diversity again.

My friend Gwen, at ninety, said humorously, "I suppose it's time I started thinking about what happens next." She also said, looking round her exquisitely chosen possessions, "The thing is, all this will still be here, but I'll be gone."

I think of that when I sit naked each morning in a hot tub placed close to the sea's edge and watch birds which come close because they do not know I'm there: scarlet-throated hummingbirds thrusting into buddleia, brilliant blue jays, once a cloud of Bohemian waxwings in migration, chickadees, an occasional hawk or eagle. From this place, I can watch and

hear seals and seal babies, the clacking of kingfishers, river otters, Canada geese, varieties of ducks, patient herons. On some
nights, the moon makes a wide swath of glittering light across
the bay. And I wonder, if I pay enough attention, if I'm mindful, can I tattoo these shapes and sounds and smells into the
fabric of myself? If I run my hand over an arbutus tree arched
over the sea, over the coolness of the new silky chartreuse skin,
over the mature warm part where it's red, over the prickliness
of the old peeling bark, will I remember it? If I draw my breath
in carefully and am mindful of the honey perfume of balm of
Gilead and the fragrance tossed into the air by wild rose leaves
before the buds have even formed, will I be able to smell it
again in my mind afterwards? Cut grass? Salt sea? The sharp,
clean odours of mint and thyme?

If I examine my hands, now veined and splotched, now
with small, hard bumps appearing on the fingers, I'm awestruck
by their ability to catch, hold, guide a pen, thread a needle,
still articulate exquisitely.

Two swans, male and female, with their four cygnets between them, one behind the other in a straight line, sail across
the bow of my canoe. The sun is setting gold and orange behind them. It is an absolutely still late afternoon. In a sense
they will still be here when I am gone. I must see them now.

The canoe is a desired possession and so is the hot tub.
Equally, a small writing room I lust after, not yet built, on the
sea's edge, could complicate rather than simplify my life. We
weight ourselves down with our possessions as well as with our
bodies. Even so, surely there is no harm in possessions if we
don't allow them to encumber us, but it takes a special skill, a
lightness, not to become enmeshed in responsibility towards

Rona Murray

things and towards people. Then we are stapled to heaviness.

One may ask why a positive "brush with death," one which suggests liberation and an explosion into previously unknown bliss, should generate passion for life, for the physical earth. Possibly we learn during such an event the truth of Jung's conclusion that all we need to do is express gratitude for such an intricate and exquisite creation. At the same time, this passion to know and remember negates the (received) knowledge that life and death are the same thing, all is one, and this richness will be with us always. There are only questions, as usual, no answers. But it is something to ask the questions. Averroës, in the twelfth century, chided his disciples, "You never formulate the final questions: Where do we come from? Where are we going? The creation, and most of all, the end and sense of life, and the history?"

With all these speculations, with this diversity and richness around us, it's astonishing how we tend towards the trivial. Terrifyingly, as we grow older and on the threshold of stepping off, we appear to become more enmeshed with insubstantial minutiae and more fearful, not of the stepping off but of what others think of us and what we think of them. Our overriding concerns so often are of how successful we've been and of how much we've achieved in comparison with others locked into the same endeavours. Who has been given a certain job, grant, honour, award? Who has made money, accumulated an inheritance to pass on after death; who has an inheritance waiting to be collected; who has brilliant and sympathetic, or not brilliant and sympathetic, children? Or, on an even more mundane level, anxiety so often increases over what we'll have for dinner and whether or not we'll be able to sleep in the coming night, over how we look, what we'll wear, how other people look, whether we need to get our hair done, how fat we are, how fat other people are, who wears a wig and who has his or her own teeth, how much our investments have gone up or down, whether we are admired and liked or not in our final hours on this astonishing planet.

As well as having an added awareness of the sweet excellence and probable uniqueness of our home, which I believe was increased by what happened to me during the car accident, I appear to be short of a buffer which once better mediated brief outbursts of temper and inappropriate remarks. My husband says I've changed, and on occasions I do explode in bursts of irritation, lack sympathy, am insensitive. Something is in me, just under the surface, which used not to be there. Possibly it is impatience: for example, over the self-conscious drama occasionally applied to death rather than the space and ritual for mourning, leave-taking, that in our society we no longer appear to possess. Time is so short. Life should be cherished, used, used up, with our eyes open. Celebrated. Then we take the next step. But I may be so callous, or lacking in understanding, I surprise myself. Those who are left behind suffer, need respect and gentleness, which to my subsequent dismay my heart has not always provided.

I comfort myself with the memory of a hermit I once knew. His name was Anton. He lived, weaving carpets from raw wool and growing vegetables for his food, isolated in the interior of British Columbia. He had built his own hut and outhouse to withstand extreme cold and heavy snowfall in winter, a burden of heat in summer. Every day he meditated, his first practice starting at three in the morning. As a Zen Buddhist and also a man of logic, he decided that if after twenty years of effort he did not break through into at least minor illumination, the system did not work.

Anton was of interest to others, particularly in the sixties when it briefly seemed as if the world might regenerate. A young man came one day to see him and talked with great sorrow about his (through newsletters) Indian guru who had "dropped his body" before coming out of a silence, self-imposed for decades. His disciples had been anxious to know what he would now communicate to them. Anton knew of the man and said robustly, "Kicked the bucket, has he? Good." That ended the conversation. At the time, but no longer, I was taken aback by his refusal to play, his honesty.

Impatience over small matters connects with the astonishment we may feel at the way fragments of the whole are treated. Most of us are appalled at what we do to each other, so there is nothing singular in my carrying around tenacious and harrowing images, but those images now have an added dimension due to the chasmic contrast between them and the knowledge of another realm in which we could be operating. Why do we begin by taunting and end by torturing and killing each other? Other animals may wound and kill for hunger or over sexual and territorial encounters, but never on the objective grounds of principle, which we invoke self-righteously when we bomb or strangle with embargoes others who are equally a part (the heart, the lungs) of the human race.

I was twenty-one when the Second World War ended and, sitting alone in a newsreel theatre in London, saw the first films to come out of Auschwitz or Buchenwald; what impressed me were not the gas chambers or the piles of skeletons, but the fragile living ghosts who stared at the camera without comprehension or reaction. They didn't appear to know what was happening and had moved far beyond any interest in outside events. Their movements were odd, in slow motion, dream. Their treatment was beyond comprehension, but it happened in a civil society. We thought it couldn't happen again. We were mistaken. Inevitably, it's the particular that clings in memory: a recent news film of a girl-child in Rwanda searching through piles of corpses after a long, lonely pilgrimage and, finding her mother and sisters in a heap of bodies, lying down without a word to die beside them.

When we are young we read, or used to read, adventure books and historical fiction; we learned of ancient times, of the iron maiden, the thumbscrew and rack, of execution by hanging a man and then drawing and quartering him. At the time, I tried to visualize a watching crowd, wondering at what point the victim actually died. It never occurred to me that we as a species were unchanged and were indeed inventing more refined tortures and methods of execution.

We are fed images of running children set on fire by bombs, of children before menses sold into prostitution, of women strapped to chairs with their knees buckled up and apart so their genitals, objects stuck in them, may be widely exposed to torture and observation. We see people deliberately burying others alive and men competing with each other to see who can, in a given time, slice off with swords the greater number of their prisoners' heads. Amputations are undertaken for amusement or justice. Mass slaughter; mass graves. Buchenwald,

Rona Murray

Nanking, Vietnam, Rwanda, Kosovo, Yugoslavia, Afghanistan.

Jonathan Swift suffered from images without journalists' reports, extensive travel, or film coverage; he watched and was aware. His Brobdingnagian king says to Gulliver: "I cannot but conclude the bulk of your natives to be the most pernicious race of little odious vermin that nature ever suffered to crawl upon the surface of the earth." His epitaph is brief: [he has gone] where fierce indignation can no longer lacerate his heart.

❦

Reactions embodying passion and disgust may have nothing to do with a car accident. However, equally, once a person has tasted, however briefly, the reverse of our hatreds and torments, our insecurities and self-imposed limitations, once he or she has glimpsed another possibility, our actions often appear not only extraordinary and cruel but also absurd. Our common litany of triviality and pain, the brokerage to which men, women, children, and animals are subject, deadens the sensibilities, but under certain circumstances the sensibilities may grow more acute. Illustrations are legion, given to us daily, of our capacity for sundering the possibility of wholeness. One may suffice, chosen for its merciless logic.

I examine again an illustration from *The Observer*, 15 June 1997, of three beautiful and modest girl-children from a poverty-stricken Pakistani family who are to be publicly beheaded if they are old enough to have started menstruating, the sign of female maturity. The mothers and aunts, some of whom are pregnant, of their extended family, nineteen people, will, in any case, be beheaded, the punishment in Saudi Arabia for drug trafficking. These tribal women and children were obliged to obey the head of their family and to swallow "eggs" of heroin in an attempt to smuggle them across the border in their stomachs or other bodily orifices. They were the paper and string of parcels.

Two of these children, eyes cast down, are swathed in head coverings and may be twelve or thirteen. Have they menstruated? Possibly. One, bare-headed, curly haired, anxiously observant, is obviously too young. What will be done with her and the babies who also travelled with this doomed family? Will this child be forced to watch the executions? Pakistan's female minister responsible for women's affairs will not intervene: justice is being observed and a powerful Muslim ally unruffled. This is a small news item, lost among thousands of other curious cases, picked out at random. Other peoples, of various religious and political persuasions, have their own stories.

We read and watch and listen, apparently impotent to change ourselves or our systems. As I write, my own "side" in a conflict, its fighting men operating in safety ten or eleven kilometres above the earth (there are no heroic medieval swords and arrows here; certainly no single combat), is dropping bombs night and day after night and day, in an attempt to destroy a small, stubborn, sovereign country that had been engaged in a desultory civil action. The leader of our alliance still insists we are not at war and that "collateral" damage is being avoided, although ant-like children far below are being blown to pieces. No doubt he feels justified in what he is doing. However, not even the most powerful and vainglorious leaders pretend to know, in a shrunken world, what the outcome will be. Part of this exquisite planet is on fire, its skies criss-crossed with death.

Rona Murray

We are flawed, standing in the medieval view between the devils and the angels. Over time we have not progressed since the biblical metaphor of a fallen Adam and Eve. Western sacred texts are far from alone in recognizing mankind's imperfections and unsuccessful struggles toward grace. One doesn't need to be formally religious; our literature is rich with examples, such as Melville's Ahab, whose long scar ran through his body like a crack through a piece of porcelain. Other traditions attempt to give other answers to the age-old question of human culpability: why? Buddhists find one explanation of our fall from grace in our taking of life in any form and thus perforating the whole. The Japanese playwright Seami Motokiyo wrote a famous nō play, *Birds of Sorrow*, based on an early legend to do with the *utō*: the seabird that hides its young for safety on the beach in sand. So well are the baby birds hidden that the parents cannot find them when they come with food; thus they cry out *"Utō"*, and the fledglings answer *"Yasukata"*. Hunters, protected by sedge-hats and straw cloaks, trace the birds by imitating these cries and then kill them for food. They need their regalia because when they unearth its young, "from the sky the parent bird [weeps] tears of blood," tears which cause sickness and death. The Chorus describes the subsequent suffering of a dead hunter who, mute, enacts its words:

> In the earthly world I thought it only an easy
> prey, this bird, only an easy prey. But now here
> in Hell it has become a gruesome phantom-
> bird, pursuing the sinner, honking from its beak

of iron, beating its mighty wings, sharpening
its claws of copper. It tears at my eyeballs, it
rends my flesh. . . . Is it not for the sin of killing
the voiceless birds that I myself now have no
voice? Is it not for slaughtering the moulting,
earth-bound birds that I cannot now flee?. . . I
have become a pheasant . . . fleeing in vain
over the earth, fearing also the sky. . . .[1]

This ancient play illustrates the web of life, the unity of
the whole and interconnectedness of every part, a proposition
current in the thinking of scientists and metaphysicians. We
are warned constantly of the "tears of blood" which bring
sickness and death if we destroy life, sully our environment
with labour-saving or money-generating poisons, rape it out of
a greed which grows more voracious the more it feeds.

There has been some change, and it rests almost entirely
with the generation that became adult in the sixties. Not long
ago, vegetarianism was considered ridiculous, unhealthy, and
a joke: an absurd, physically dangerous practice. Today it is
common. "Ecology" is a recently familiar addition to the non-
scientific vocabulary. I've been told by a generous investor in
conservationist causes that many computer systems'
millionaires, whose wealth—like his own—has come out of
Silicon Valley, are now intimately and without publicity
connected to environmental causes. Young men and women
have proved they are willing to lay their lives on the line to
protect sea life, botanical sanctuaries, and animals. They are
fortunate individuals who have found a constructive cause which

Rona Murray

may take the place, in some instances, of religious ethics and regulated charity.

※

Notwithstanding our largely unsuccessful attempts to understand what we are and why we behave the way we do, and whether or not we are something more than intricate biological machines, we do harbour the dream of a different reality, seen perhaps through a brush with death, through a whirling dervish dance, mind-altering drugs, meditation, or the self-immolating passion for a deity, place, or person which leads to wholeness.

Having experienced the possibility of that other reality, whether through personal experience or through messengers we may or may not recognize (such as, for example, the swans in Plato's *Phaedo*), our brief awareness may give us a kick forward: an indication of further journeying towards what is, in our present state of consciousness, the unimaginable.

Plato's swans, strange messengers to choose since they are not known to sing, divine another, more joyful world to come; but if that world and this are indivisible, as many ancient and modern teachers insist, we should be at home in that part of it which is our rightful heritage—here:

> Do you think I have less divination than the
> swans? For they, when they know that they
> must die, having sung all their lives sing louder
> than ever, for joy at going home to the god
> they serve. Men, who themselves fear death,
> have taken it for lamentation, forgetting no

bird sings in hunger, or cold, or pain. But being Apollo's, they share his gift of prophecy, and foresee the joys of another world. . . .

CELEBRANT

Each one

the holy mariners
dip their oars
in the same
instant

In the same
instant
water drips
from their oars
in the sun

I stare out
to sea

pick
seed heads
from magenta nasturtiums
tattered now
when evening comes

WORDS MAY BE INADEQUATE, or at least sentence structure may make it difficult, to say what one wants to say. Sometimes it is simpler to express the non-objective through poems. Poetry hints, suggests, rather than states; the form does not demand absolute and logical explication. It is not attempting to instruct, but to leaven the imagination. I'm going to invoke it. What I'm attempting is not empirical, and needs non-empirical language.

Hence the poem above. I puzzle over its meaning. It was written before my accident but I think it is in touch with the space of that experience. It appeared in my head one day while I was deadheading nasturtiums and stopped for a moment to look out to sea, vaguely aware of conifers, rocky islands, lazy seals. The abstracted (absent) state I entered used to be called a "brown study." It's not unusual. Children fall into brown studies and are chided for lack of attention to the here and now. For me, it's all too usual: the reason friends won't drive with me at the wheel. This is an absolute disadvantage in our usual lives; however, I've heard one is apparently more likely to encounter a transformative experience if subject to brown studies. In this, it seems to me, that habit is an advantage.

Where are we when we are not actually here or when we are sleeping? We may be partially *there*. Somewhere else. The poem seems to be saying time is coexistent, not linear, nothing is lost, and another world interacts with ours, possibly on a different rate of vibration. Canadian poet Patricia Young in an enchanting poem about the absent experience says: "I was conscious as a tree is conscious./ Like a stone I simply was." She calls her poem "Three Days Before Christmas":

Three days before Christmas and a rock-opera
rendition of *Silent Night* was playing
on the car radio. Beside me
my son hummed along, his friends
slouched down in the back, their faces
vacant, just glad to be going
somewhere, anywhere, a rec centre
with a chlorinated pool. I was driving
past the sea wall thinking
I'd drop them off
then stop on my way home
for bagels and bananas when a hand
reached out of the sky and rested on my shoulder.
All was calm. I remember
the day was unseasonably mild, that sunlight
haloed the cherry trees
blooming too early along the winding
coast road, I remember liking
the rock opera rendition of *Silent Night*, also
my son and his friends, the way
they hunched over the towels in their laps
as though the Christ-child himself
were jelly-rolled inside. All the same,
how explain that sudden peace?
I was conscious as a tree is conscious.
Like a stone I simply was.
And then the station-wagon was a riotous belly
emptying itself of eleven-year-old boys.
The hand lifted, the sky slammed shut.
I was myself again, a woman with greying hair

sitting in a parking lot
watching three boys swish down
a sidewalk in T-shirts and jeans so enormous
they might have been small,
fine-boned angels
shuffling toward
the bright waters of heaven.

Both poems move into a clarifying space, a sudden quietness where metaphorical angels may hover, and both hint at a
possibility of the further space entered during transcendental
transformation, the oneness of consciousness I have been attempting to describe.

That experience, and more particularly its aftermath once
the inquiring mind is wakened, reinforces our held breath and
astonishment at the richness, kindness, and diversity of our
earth, particularly in its living organisms from the largest to
the smallest. By the same token, the more aware any one of us
becomes and the more we celebrate the earth, the more aware
we also become of its shadow side: our destructive capabilities.

Since the introduction of drawing on cave walls and of
devising an alphabet, men chiefly, because they had the tools,
and women occasionally have recorded their wonder at the
earth's diversity: at, for example, the sheer size and strength of
leviathan. "He maketh the deep to boil like a pot: he maketh
the sea like a pot of ointment. He maketh a path to shine after
him; one would think the deep to be hoary" (Job 41:31–32).
Later, in *The Bestiary*, a medieval monk must have amused himself likening the whale to the devil in its destructive powers.

Ships that are storm driven "look about them, and see this fish":

> An island they suppose it is.
> For that they are deeply grateful,
> And with all their might thereto they draw
> The ship to anchor,
> And they all go ashore.
> From stone and steel in the tinder
> They kindle a fire on this monster;
> They warm them well and eat and drink.
> The fire he feeleth and maketh them sink;
> At once he diveth to the ground,
> And destroyeth them all without a wound.

Herman Melville, awestruck by the dimensions, strength, amplitude, and commercial usefulness of sperm whales, believed they could not be wiped out. He was mistaken. Only recently have we begun to realize that all wild creatures may be destroyed by those who were given "dominion" over them, who were relegated to care for them.

In this century a start has been made toward unravelling the mystery of the whale. Even so, a subterranean awe still exists and is not unjustified. It is as well we may recognize how puny we are without the force of weapons devised by our heads, not our hearts.

The blue whale, over eighty feet in length, eats four tons of krill, if available, a day; its calves, born at intervals of two to three years, are twenty-seven feet long and three tons in weight at birth. Once Sven Foyn invented the exploding harpoon gun and factory boats, 29,000 blue whale were harvested in one season. So few of this once-sociable creature now exist, it is known as the lonely whale, roaming the seas for a mate which may not be found.

Killer whales (orca), on the other hand, are familial. They live in pods and exhilarate in skill when hunting in packs:

Looking lonely
for shells
my daughter

looking lonely for shells
she walked
into the black of the cliff

waves poured onto lava fists

in pools
barnacles extended threads of tongues
crabs
—lidless eyes intent—
slithered out
        of their dark

and out and out
killer whales gouging chunks of flesh
from the spent and thrashing blue whale's flank
leaped
in a sea of blood.

A man flying in his small plane over the sea watched this death and told me the water was stained with blood in an ever widening circle, a mile or so in diameter, around the protagonists.

Now we know more about whales, we also know they are remarkably intelligent and are able to communicate with each other over considerable distances, possibly telepathically. The blue's deep rumble allows it to give signals or converse over hundreds of miles of ocean. The orca remain in the vicinity of the pool, if that is physically possible, in which one of their pod is imprisoned after capture. Communally, they nurture and guard their young.

I live on the west coast of British Columbia, along which great grey whales migrate, returning from Mexico, and where orca are resident in their pods. This coast, where many logging camps are accessible only by boat or plane, is famous for its giant Douglas firs and cedars. In one such camp, the loggers, as they released the enormous corpses of trees into a small bay for shipping in booms, targeted a pod of resident whales. Their sport was to see how many they could hit. One calm summer evening, several took out a power boat to visit a coastal beer parlour and disappeared without a trace. It was firmly believed (loggers, of course, may be superstitious) that the whales with their mysterious powers had taken revenge. Obversely, Aboriginal peoples trust whales will present themselves to be slaughtered when the time is ripe and the hunters have cleansed and purified themselves for their spiritual quest. If we could enter into the minds of these creatures (of course, we can't even enter into each other's minds) what would we find there?

Orca are like athletic men in tails, dancing: with sharply

demarcated black and white skin, they leap and twist out of the water, flick their tails when they dive into the depths. They are gentle (unless in search of food), and apart from the possible incident recounted above have never been known in the wild to attack a human. One night a young friend of mine, Michelle, sat alone on a pebbled beach, part of Malcolm Island, looking across the shimmering Pacific at the moon and diminished stars. A pod of whales rushed at the shore within ten feet of her, reared up, glittering wet white and black in the moonlight. She was stunned and sat there, astonished and without harm. They came again and again. Later she was told she was sitting in their space, one of the areas to which they come in order to scrape against the stones and cleanse their bellies of anything which clings to them.

D. H. Lawrence, in his ecstatic poem "Whales Weep Not!", best expresses the magnitude and mystery of this world off our shores and beneath our ships when he writes of blissful union and of Cherubim, signifying wisdom, which attend the whales' rituals:

> And over the bridge of the whale's strong phallus,
> > linking the wonder of whales
> the burning archangels under the sea keep passing, back
> > and forth,
> keep passing archangels of bliss
> from him to her, from her to him, great Cherubim
> that wait on whales in mid-ocean, suspended in the waves
> > of the sea
> great heaven of whales in the waters, old hierarchies.
> And enormous mother whales lie dreaming suckling their

whale-tender young
and dreaming with strange whale eyes wide open in the
waters of the beginning and the end.

Lawrence feels the whale. The chances are he knew nothing of its anatomical features, of its teeth or baleen, its length, skin, weight, type, classification. But he knew its mystery, and that is what we are in danger of losing or ignoring in a society where we clone animals, seen as objects only, and where we will no doubt in time clone humans, seen also as objects; where we interfere for our ease and profit with the chemistry of living creatures and experiment genetically with the generous fruits of the loam we stand on. We misuse the earth—perhaps one day she will turn over and throw us, irritating fleas, overboard— by objectifying her, separating her from ourselves. Indigenous peoples around the world know this; we, technologically so successful, appear to have forgotten it. Multiple production, cloning, regarding animals and humans as objects may be seen as the reverse of the order in which members of a species such as the whale gather at a birth to lift tenderly one of their own so it might breathe living air. And we are all, every one of us, unique.

If we move from the largest living animal, the ninety-foot whale, to the (presumably) smallest unit of matter, we are told by scientists that each of us is individually constructed of singular material. If in his poem, Lawrence "feels" the mystery of the whale, the mystery of the cell is at least as astonishing.

Since the invention of the microscope, men and women have been discovering just how each fragment of life contains the whole, each cell forming a self-sufficient factory able to "hydrolyse, oxidise, pull to pieces and build up, according to its needs; it can even manufacture its own special proteins from the proteins that it has absorbed from without" (Walker). Cells have the power to heal themselves if damaged or afflicted, to grow and move independently in Petri dishes. Each contains all that is needed for an entire physical structure; each is a reflection of the whole and is unmatched, outside its own body, in its DNA.

Late in the 1960s I was visiting a cousin near Oxford. She introduced me to the president, at that time, of the Box Society. This woman was friendly, well educated, upper middle class, dressed in tweeds and brogues: the epitome of her country and class. She invited us to see the "boxes" in operation, saying she did not know how they worked but knew they did. She appeared to me, in my ignorance, similar in her eccentricity to members of the Flat Earth Society: pleasant and mad.

In her "laboratory" many black boxes were placed in rows on small tables. Each was fronted with a strip of rough material which, when it was stroked, activated treatment for a specific affliction in a specific entity. The patients' names were displayed above their private boxes containing a sample of hair or skin or nail; the names often appeared to belong to members of the aristocracy (Lady Bessington) or to animals, particularly dogs or cows (Rex, Bessie). We were told the patient could reside at any distance. He or she or it would be found by the box.

My cousin, who prided herself on her psychic ability, stroked a piece of material, generating friction, and instantly a needle on a dial shot into action. When I stroked a strip little happened. Perhaps that is why, in lacking psychic gifts, I found the whole operation absurd. Even so, it was interesting to speculate on the connection between this simple apparatus, with its claims to locate and treat a patient through cellular fragments, and a shaman's or witch's use of the same kinds of material. It is no longer so easy to mock old wives' tales, tribal manipulations, or eccentric Englishwomen now that we know the DNA in each fragment stipulates an individual and distinct human or animal.

What extraordinary mind expansion we experience if we celebrate the possibility that every cell and cellular structure is differentiated, contains seeds of the whole, and at the same time is part of a vast universe of equally differentiated stars and planets singing their transcendent paths through and within not only our known cosmos, but also others astrophysicists are newly discovering: every item, whether magnificent beyond comprehension or minute, from the whale to the cell, individual and of value.

> Are not five sparrows sold for two farthings?
> and not one of them is forgotten before God:
> But even the very hairs of your head are all
> numbered. Fear not, therefore: ye are of more
> value than many sparrows. (Luke 12:6–7)

This is a harmonious view of creation: one which suggests it is more practical and advantageous to recognize ourselves as part of a vast web, in our rightful places, flowing with the rhythms of the universe as the whales flow with the rhythms of the seas and the migratory birds with the seasons, rather than to live, as we tend to do, within a laager, rigid in our expectations. None of us knows how to flow, unafraid, in this way, imprinted, patterned, and shaped as we are.

Stargazer Chet Raymo, in *The Soul of the Night*, reinforces with wildly excited language and image his vision of the atom, the cosmos, the co-dependence and constant flux in which he suggests we exist.

> Every atom of the Earth, excepting the hydrogen and some of the helium, was made in the hot core of a star or in the energetic convulsions that accompany the end of the star's life. Every carbon atom in the graphite of the pencil I write with carries a label that says "Made in Taurus" or "Made in Orion." The universe burns. The atoms flow out of stars and across galaxies—now they are dust in the Horsehead Nebula of Orion, now they are the crust of a new planet—like circulating coins or baseball cards, trading hands. The atoms flow through the body of the mourning cloak [butterfly] and pause only briefly, in and out with every breath. Every second the entire surface of the Earth goes into a pupa and rearranges its form. "The sun is new each day," said Heraclitus. Did he mean it literally? "The thunderbolt steers all things," he said. The universe is afire, kindling in measure and going out in measure. Step in the river and burn your foot. Step in the same river and burn the same foot

Rona Murray

and it is neither the same river nor the same foot.

Most of us are not astronomers, but we can all look up at the night sky, remembering, if we care to, that the ancients thought a cosmic bowl covered the earth, and the stars and moon shone through its interstices, indicating the brilliance outside a tent of darkness. During the penultimate February of this millennium, Venus and Jupiter, the two brightest planets in the night sky, almost conjoined in that they were so close they appeared in the same telescopic field of view; actually they were still 600 million kilometres apart. But who could think of that when a thin crescent moon hovered close, three glittering jewels in the westering face of night: the grace of the moment, the held breath.

Once I kept bees, not very successfully but with enthusiasm. This was long before I was considering uniqueness, individual difference, metaphysical value. But eventually, slowly, all comes together. Before discovering my violent allergic reaction to the sting, I would sit for long summer stretches in a bathing suit in front of the hives, watching a glass observation unit with its queen, pampered by worker bees bringing in nectar and pollen, as she busied herself laying her thousands of eggs, indifferent to drones lazing on the front step. I knew bee stings were said to cure asthma, and honey to cure hay fever if taken internally, acne and dreaded skin ailments if externally. I had also read that no bacteria may exist in honey and that the perfect corpses of Egyptian babies, over four or five thousand years old, had been found preserved in honeyed amphora. It wasn't surprising to me then—I simply accepted it—that each hive manufactured a singular fragrance, every one idiosyncratic so that intruders from another hive and robber wasps might be at once identified. Now I think, how do they do it? Each colony is as unique as each whale, star, cell, individual.

> Hives, aromatic with propolis
> from poplar trees and liquid honey,
> house bees that smell of various roses,
> each skep distinct to warn of trespassers,
> each fuelled by fanning wings
> planted over glands set in
> a hundred thousand abdomens.

To return to the Canadian doctor Richard Bucke and his treatise on what he called cosmic consciousness, he suggested that distinguishing—actually seeing and smelling—colours and fragrances arrived very late in human development. His speculation is based on reading epic poetry such as the *Iliad* and the *Odyssey*, the Vedas, and (partially) the Bible with their lack of references to these earthy physical characteristics. For example, "blue" sky is never identified and no fragrances are mentioned until we arrive at *The Song of Songs*. Now colour blindness, affecting to a greater or lesser degree forty-seven per cent of the population, is considered an atavistic throwback. Bucke speculates that over the centuries, as we evolved, the ability to see colour and to recognize odour expanded, and now, similarly, as the species evolves, more and more individuals will experience a new level of consciousness: one that is enlightening and helpful in breaking our old destructive patterns. Judging by the numbers of people (they have even formed societies) who have had or at least claim to have had out-of-body or near-death or transcendental experiences which have proved to be blissful and mind altering, his supposition may be fruitful. This possible evolutionary development may be linked to a new sense like the Hindu third eye, a new seeing, of recognizing we are an integral part of a single whole and together we create our universe.

The modern Brahmin philosopher, Krishnamurti, based his entire teaching on our need to de-imprint ourselves and celebrate reality rather than to accept appearances, having been taught falsely. His purpose was to set us free from the fears, limitations, and greed which separate us, and to force us to take responsibility for the ugly physical and spiritual dishar-mony we have created. At one with the quantum physicists and their putative universe consisting of energy-generating connections and thought patterns, Krishnamurti implicitly said: "We are the world," and Plotinus, third-century mystic, "Each being contains in itself the whole intelligible world. Therefore All is everywhere."

Equally, the Burmese practice of *vipassana* meditation—a process of attention to the moment by moment experience of one's life—is based on the theory that we are not set, solid objects but are in a continuous state of flux. Only by paying minute attention to the five senses and to the rest of the body (each breath, muscle ache, itch, desire to sneeze or cough) may we strip away the conditioning that has taken place since our birth.

Perhaps in general the closest we come to the ecstatic experience, whatever its cause, lies in those moments when we are physically and spiritually so close to another being, to union, that we literally appear to meld into that person, or when we are in love with the earth, with the universe, or, for mystics, with God. "Every love is a wish for union" (Ibn Arabi) which leads to wholeness. To move into this knowledge of love requires us to escape all impediments and distractions. For most of us, the experience is fleeting, without expectation, not to be recalled except as a memory of its having been. However, the memory alone brings with it a flush of gratitude. This lovely sensation is not dependent on an accident, a drug, a whirling dance, nor on increased consciousness or mysterious enlightenment, but carries with it the same harmonious oneness that they do, and the same recognition of an underlying sweetness in our physical universe.

Gerard Manley Hopkins, a Jesuit who was prone to debilitating depression and who felt himself a failure at everything he turned his hand to, lived and worked in the slums in England during the Industrial Revolution. The natural world was wounded with poverty, mean streets, steam and smoke, dirt, garbage, and lack of care in the industrialized nations even more than it is today, although not on such a worldwide scale. Hopkins, an artist and musician as well as a poet, hated the stench and destruction of the environment but sensed always an enfolding harmony cradling the universe. He expressed his passionate love for the earth and for his God, nurtured by his belief in the Roman Catholic doctrine, in everything he wrote; for example, in "God's Grandeur":

The world is charged with the grandeur of God.
  It will flame out, like shining from shook foil;
  It gathers to a greatness, like the ooze of oil
Crushed. Why do men then now not reck his rod?
Generations have trod, have trod, have trod;
  And all is seared with trade; bleared, smeared with toil;
  And wears man's smudge and shares man's smell: the soil
Is bare now, nor can foot feel, being shod.

And for all this, nature is never spent;
  There lives the dearest freshness deep down things;
And though the last lights off the black west went
  Oh, morning, at the brown brink eastward, springs—
Because the Holy Ghost over the bent
  World broods with warm breast and with ah! bright wings.

"There lives the dearest freshness deep down things": we don't need to subscribe to a specific doctrine to be aware of this restorative sweetness or to respond to the image of an unencumbered presence sheltering our earth under great, nurturing wings. It is over a hundred years since Hopkins wrote this sonnet. As caretakers of the planet, we have not improved, but as ecologists, gardeners, environmentalists, lovers, we respond, achingly aware of our world's beauty and fragility as well as of our intimate connection with the whole.

This love experience in whatever form and its contingent need to find union with the beloved, the knowledge of disrupted oneness, hinted in personal relationships or passions, often appears in poetry as excruciating loss: our angst lies in our separateness. The "other" has disappeared, is known to exist but cannot be found. Experiencing desolation, Hopkins writes "my lament/ Is cries countless, cries like dead letters sent/ To dearest him that lives alas! away." Saint John of the Cross speaks of this dread separation, of being abandoned by God, in *The Dark Night of the Soul* (a much misused term today). Satan, in *Paradise Lost*, bemoans a punishment which is entirely endurable except for his separation from God. The twelfth-century *bhakti* poet, Mahadeviyakka, writes of her self-immolating search for Shiva who has been hidden from her through countless incarnations:

> Not one, not two, not three or four,
> but through eighty-four hundred thousand vaginas
> have I come,
>   I have come
> through unlikely worlds,
>   guzzled on
> pleasure and pain.
>   Whatever be
> all previous lives,
>   show me mercy
> this one day
>   O lord
>   white as jasmine[2]

Mahadeviyakka knew Shiva to be in all things, but to be, in her loneliness for her lover, absent: "You are the forest/ you are all the great trees/ in the forest/ you are bird and beast/

playing in and out/ of all the trees/ O Lord white as jasmine/
filling and filled by all/ why don't you/ show me your face?"

Her passionate desire for unity and her knowledge of separation, like that of Hopkins, expresses itself through her
attachment to a specific deity but is also a lament for the fragmented universe in which we live, symbolized in biblical
literature as the Fall, when we were cast out of the garden (the
"oneness"?), and thus were truncated, a severing resulting in
loneliness and its supposed cure: acquisition in all its forms.

Mahadeviyakka died scarcely into her twenties. An ecstatic,
a rebel, she discarded everything, including her clothing, and
wrapped in her hair wandered through India searching for
union.

The great German poet Rilke, in the *Duino Elegies*, writes
poignantly of the exile's memory of wholeness, his hunger, his
knowledge of loss:

> Yet in the alert, warm animal there lies
> the pain and burden of an enormous sadness.
> For it too feels the presence of what often
> overwhelms us: a memory, as if
> the element we keep pressing toward was once
> more intimate, more true, and our communion
> infinitely tender. Here all is distance;
> there it was breath. After that first home,
> the second seems ambiguous and drafty. ("Eighth Elegy")

Later, in the "Ninth Elegy," his longing toward wholeness
is a recognition that if one has ever experienced non-separation,

it is always known: "But to have been/ this once, completely, even if only once:/ to have been at one with the earth, seems beyond undoing."

Rumi, thirteenth century, was born in Afghanistan, but spent his life in Konya, Turkey, where he headed the dervish community. He too was unpredictable, eccentric, lost in passion, careless of his appearance, a searcher for his Friend who had "disappeared." Finally, he realizes, "Why should I seek? I am the same as/ he. His essence speaks through me./ I have been looking for myself!" Rumi uses the tavern as a metaphor. It is filled with delightful wines, companionship, confusion, and wantings. After some time "a point comes, a memory of elsewhere, a longing for the source, and the drunks must set off from the tavern and begin the return. . . . A breaking apart, a crying out in the street, begins in the tavern, and the human soul turns to find its way home." Home is union, completion, not a physical place.

> If I separated myself from you,
> I would turn entirely thorn.
>
> Every second I drink another cup of my own blood-wine.
> Every instant, I break an empty cup against your door.
>
> I reach out, wanting you to tear me open.
>
> Saladin's generosity lights a candle in my chest.
> Who *am* I then?
> > His empty begging bowl.

Equally, Rumi uses death as a metaphor for new knowledge:

Inside this new love, die.
Your way begins on the other side.
Become the sky.
Take an axe to the prison wall.
Escape.
Walk out like someone suddenly born into color.
Do it now.
You're covered with thick cloud.
Slide out the side. Die,
and be quiet. Quietness is the surest sign
that you've died.
Your old life was a frantic running
from silence.

The speechless full moon
comes out now.

Francis Thompson (1859–1907), a misfit who lived a fragile and spasmodic life, was to all appearances a total failure. It appears that these poets, lost in another world, found it almost impossible to fit into this one. Louis Untermeyer writes of Thompson:

His attempts to earn a living were a succession of failures. He was employed as a book-agent, and sold no books; he was apprenticed to the boot trade, and spent many hours of his apprenticeship in public libraries; he enlisted as a soldier, and was discharged as incompetent. He went to London, as Francis Meynell says: "not so much to seek his fortune as to escape his bad fortune. He lost in the gamble, but literature gained. He lived for four years as errand man, seller of matches, holder of horses' heads. Soon he became too shabby to gain admittance into the public libraries, so that when one says the desire of reading was with him a passion, one restores to its literal meaning that abused word. He slept on the Embankment, and 'saw the traffic of Jacob's ladder pitched betwixt Heaven and Charing Cross.' A woman of the streets took pity on him and kept him alive by her charity. . . . He began to write—now for the first time. His poem, "Dream Tryst", written on blue sugar wrapping, found after many months an editorial welcome. Thereafter he was persuaded to come off the streets; and even to give up for many years the laudanum he had been taking."

Thompson, like Mahadeviyakka, cared little for normal needs and appearances because he was consumed by another reality. It is easy for us to consider them both as well as Rumi, Blake, the medieval mystic Suso, and many others as pathological simply because they are not like us. Where we see separation and categories, Thompson saw physical and

68   *Rona Murray*

spiritual unity, every part linked and co-dependent: ". . . thou canst not stir a flower/ without troubling of a star"; "The drift of pinion, would we hearken,/ beats at our own clay-shuttered doors"; "The angels keep their ancient places; turn but a stone and start a wing!" Christ walks timelessly on the water, "not of Gennesareth, but Thames!" Blake, who was said by his wife to hold daily conversations with poets of the past, had the same kind of vision: "To see a world in a grain of sand/ And a heaven in a wild flower," as well as feeling fury over ruptures in the membrane of wholeness.

We have few words to express what is little understood or known, so mystics and poets find physical love, which most of us have experienced, as the nearest equivalent through which they can express their need for union with the "other" or their sense of "elsewhere". In "The Hound of Heaven," Thompson flees from rather than pines for God, only finally to be caught. Perhaps we are all fleeing, except in those moments when we are truly awake:

> I fled Him, down the nights and down the days;
>   I fled Him, down the arches of the years;
> I fled Him down the labyrinthine ways
>   Of my own mind; and in the midst of tears
> I hid from Him, and under running laughter.
>   Up vistaed hopes I sped;
>   And shot, precipitated,
> Adown Titanic glooms of chasmed fears,
>   From those strong Feet that followed, followed after.
>   But with unhurrying chase,
>   And unperturbed pace,

Deliberate speed, majestic instancy,
  They beat—and a Voice beat
  More instant than the Feet—
"All things betray thee, who betrayest Me."

.   .   .   .

  Halts by me that footfall:
  Is my gloom, after all,
Shade of his hand, outstretched caressingly?
  "Ah, fondest, blindest, weakest,
  I am He Whom thou seekest!
Thou dravest love from thee, who dravest Me."[3]

Today we may be uncomfortable with the Victorian language, the capital letters, the exclamation marks, the anthropomorphic, personal god, but it's not possible to doubt the passion. The simplicity of Rumi, who has the advantage of contemporary translation, is closer to modern taste ("when I was apart from you,/ this world did not exist,/ nor any other"), but they are both saying the same thing: our view is fragmented, is not really; union, love, is desired as much by the tenacious "Hound" as it is by us.

I spent years in a stoically Anglican boarding school, where passion could exist only, if it did, surreptitiously. The single book we were allowed to keep in our cubicles was the Bible. Perhaps because it was "holy" it appeared so boring there was not much danger of our reading it. Even so, we were given the usual explanation that the "Song of Solomon" is an allegory depicting the love of Christ for his church. Hard to imagine. Apart from the obvious difficulties in historical time, according to the gospels, Jesus was not in the least interested in establishing a church. It appears more likely, of course, that Solomon was singing of Sheba or, at times, Sheba of Solomon. But perhaps it celebrates the Self's longing for God, and God's longing for the Self: union. At any rate, a beautiful sexual poem, it may also be regarded as another hymn composed in a heightened state of spiritual rapture. It makes little difference if the outpouring is sacred or sexual when the desire is the desire for wholeness:

> As the lily among the thorns, so is my love among the daughters. As the apple tree among the trees of the wood, so is my beloved among the sons. I sat down under his shadow with great delight, and his fruit was sweet to my taste. He brought me to the banqueting house, and his banner over me was love. Stay me with flagons, comfort me with apples; for I am sick of love. . . . O my dove, that art in the clefts of the rock, in the secret places of the stairs, let me see thy countenance, let me hear thy voice; for sweet is thy voice, and thy countenance is comely. . . . By night on my bed I sought him whom my soul loveth: I sought him but I found him not. I will arise now, and go about the city in the streets, and in the broad ways I will seek him whom my soul loveth. . . .

"My love" is hidden in the clefts of the rocks and in the

secret places; the other is everywhere but cannot be found.

One of my favourite accounts, a gentle and humorous rendering by Evelyn Underhill, is the story, drawn from his autobiography, of medieval Suso. Above all, Suso desired to be a chivalrous knight in his great and passionate love for God. When God withdrew from him and he was forced to endure not only spiritual poverty but also social condemnation, having been accused maliciously of fathering a child, he cried out piteously: "And may one not weep, and show that one is hurt, when one is hit very hard?" His visions give him no mercy; he is told impatiently *Viriliter agita!* (Be a man!):

> Suso was visited by fresh trials: and soon forgetting his valiant declarations, he began as usual to complain of his griefs. The result was a visionary ecstasy, always attributed a divine validity, inquiring with ill-concealed irony, "Well, what has become of that noble chivalry? Who is this knight of straw, this rag-made man? It is not by making rash promises and drawing back when suffering comes, that man wins the ring of Eternity which you desire."
>
> "Alas! Lord," Suso said plaintively, "the tournaments in which one must suffer for Thee last such a very long time!"

After more trials, Suso writes of himself, "His feeble nature broken by the pains which he had to endure, he went forth raving like one who has lost his senses; and hid himself in a place far from men, where none could see or hear him." Having finally learned that he can obtain unity ("dwell in the Ocean of Divine Love") only by becoming completely human, not fearing the world and its calumny, Suso declares, "If it cannot be otherwise, *fiat voluntas tua* [thy will be done] . . . and in the event, God came to the help of the Servitor, and little by little that terrible tempest died away." Later, he describes the end of the quest, not as extinction of the human personality but as transcendence: "When the good and faithful servant enters into the joy of his Lord, he feels . . . in an ineffable degree, that which is felt by an inebriated man. He forgets himself, he is no longer conscious of his selfhood; he disappears and loses himself . . . as a drop of water which is drowned in a great quantity of wine."

The brief contemporary experiences we have come to know as being "out of body" have nothing, so far as can be ascertained, to do with the tumultuous spiritual quests and hunger (would modern psychology regard these individuals as being manic-depressives?) of recognized mystics. Even so, there is a similarity in the actual experience, just as there is with that of epileptics subsumed by their "holy" malady: the joy felt "in an ineffable degree," the merging of a still-intact personal self with an Otherness generating love or bliss. Suso does not mention some further characteristics: a yearning to know again that ecstasy, loss of a fear of death, the bright light most acknowledge, or encounters with spiritual beings and/or angelic figures, although in his visions he is given disciplinary measures by a "magnificent knight" as he struggles along his desired journey.

The concept of unity, the hunger to defeat separation, may be reinforced by this century's theory of chaos: that each fragment on the planet (not excepting the hypothetical possibility, or probability, that the whole may extend beyond this planet) is tied together so closely each one affects the rest: when one thing happens, another (its ghostly reflection?) will also occur. The usual and simplistic example given is that of the butterfly which beats its wings in Brazil and thus generates a typhoon in Hawaii. More specifically, the theory devised by American physicist Mitchell Feigenbaum is that of consistent patterns of rate-doubling as a system tends toward chaos. If there is any truth in the mathematical theory which supports this connectedness,[4] every time we empty ourselves of ourselves and experience love, and every time we wound anyone or any aspect of creation, the emotion or action expands, until we are effectively loving or wounding the whole.

Certainly, when we are in love, when we experience that spellbinding euphoria which blinds us to so much, we at the same time become aware that the delight in our hearts overflows, encompassing the earth around us and everything it contains. The most ordinary, unloved wastelands are for the moment transformed. Similarly, when a small child is raped and torn, animals caged and tortured, the earth irreparably damaged, we feel the reverberations in ourselves.

Not long ago, my sister met an American Buddhist whose beloved daughter had died suddenly in a car crash. This woman did not grieve. She said she had seen her daughter take off on her journey ecstatic with joy, still, or possibly more, a part of the whole than when "alive". Some years ago, a man I knew, Brent, died of AIDS. He loved people, was a warm host, superb cook, enthusiastic gardener, generous friend. He gave me many plants, shared tapes and books. In his kitchen, preparing an exotic meal, Thai or Turkish or some new concoction, he was relaxed as he stirred the enchanting odours in his clay pots and woks while discussing novels and poems and films. His presence was with us after his departure. We all are aware of the ghostly essences, generally for a short time, of some of those who have gone. These essences may only exist in our imaginations, in a kind of peripheral vision. They may not be "real" in our sense of the word; equally, there may, with some, be a lingering vibration. For Brent:

> Melancholy gentlemen are blooming now,
> but sparsely, as if they know the man
> whose garden they came from has gone,
> sent forth from a Catholic church to which
> gardeners across the city brought
> choice buds, stripping blooms and foliage
> from plants.
>
> Hardy geraniums have flowered, defiant
> hen and chickens thrust out starry blooms,
> asters in a dozen colours wait out
> summer's heat—all gifts from one
> who instructed me in lineage and
> habitat.
>
> First blindness. His hand lightly on my arm,
> I led him round his garden; each location,
> variety, and history locked into his mind—

happy accidents, careful crosses, stories
of queens and desperate empresses who nurtured
plants with lutes and fountains in their
walled enclosures.

He loved the small—secrets hidden in
shade of shrub, serrated fern, simple moss.
Netsuke in his house.

Then his brain: intricate knowledge lost.
His heart remained faithful to the end. A Jew
he chose conversion: "I want to be in heaven
with my friend."

His friend, small and delicate as netsuke
had chosen heavyheaded rhododendrons
for a garden which wept rain on the day
we ate rich food, drank champagne,
in celebration of a ghostly figure
passing through the bubbles of our
conversation.

His friend will go with him,
and soon.

Flowers. Joy. Love. Interconnection. Celebration. The breakthrough that happens suddenly and with no warning, without expectation and conscious seeking, all remind me of a small section in a dissertation, a copy of which was given to

R o n a   M u r r a y

me recently by the author, Philo Hove, candidate for a doctorate. He had recorded an interview with a woman, identified as Shelley, made during a retreat:

> I wanted to tell you about having an experience of joy. I wasn't really sure if I should tell anyone and then I decided to tell you because you might understand, but I don't know if I'd want to share this with everyone quite yet. Just before the group walking this morning, at the same moment when the bell was released I was struck by this intense feeling of pure joy. . . . It's like the joy you get from looking at a flower sometimes, only here it was like the joy of looking at all the flowers in the world . . . concentrated into a single instance. . . . This has never happened to me before.
>
> The whole world of effort and worries just dissolved. . . . I feel so light now. . . . Nothing led up to it . . . it was really indescribable . . . but it also seems very familiar somehow.

Shelley did not lose the sense of transformation. Weeks later, and then a month further on, it was with her, until finally she felt as if her ego was too attached to the experience and she could let it go, accept it as a part of herself:

> It's like I've been struck by lightning, the effect it's had on my life. I've lost all sense of

the future. Now there's this wonderful sense of living moment by moment. Usually my days would be pretty up and down, but now there's this equanimity; things have lost their intensity. . . . It's almost as if I'm ready to die, like there's no difference between life and death. I don't feel attached to anything, no grasping or clinging. I still love my family of course but now it's different somehow. . . .

Re-reading the account of my experience . . . made me realize that I had left out one important aspect when I first told you. I did not realize until much later that this was really the essence of the experience. When the bell sparked the explosion or release (words seem very inadequate) mind and body seemed to dissolve and my first thought was "This is why I have been sitting here [in meditation]." Later I asked myself why that was my first thought. Why had I been sitting there? What was it I suddenly knew? Now I realize that suddenly I knew that I am a part of everything and everything is a part of me. Also I am nothing and do not exist. It was a coming to zero. Everything is interconnected.

And then the joy flooded me. The joy was overwhelming and seemed to obscure that brief instant when I came to zero.

I remembered, when I read this description, my own unex-

Rona Murray

pected spurt of joy some years ago when the Dalai Lama visited my town. It had nothing to do in any way with the revelation during the car accident and certainly was not as defined or as lasting as that one, but a totally unexpected swoosh just the same. To be truthful, I had forgotten this small gift (do we all forget these moments when something out of the ordinary happens, and do we forget them because we are not ready for them?) until I went through papers looking for the prayer of the *Brahma Viharas* given to me when a friend introduced me to forms of Tibetan Buddhism, because something in Shelley's words ("I don't feel attached to anything. . . . I still love my family, of course, but now it's different. . . .") reminded me of this partial invocation to be repeated at the beginning and end of meditation: "May all leave attachments to dear ones and aversion to others and live believing in the equalness of all that lives."

Perhaps now I have unexpectedly found my piece of paper with the title "Jottings," noting the rush of joy, I may as well use it if only because I am flirting with Jung's theory of synchronicity: the felicitous coming together. This account was written simply as a record and now reminds me of the lack of self-consciousness and self-importance of the Buddhist monks who visited Victoria some years ago, of their casualness:

> Jump of joy. Not jump for joy. But a
> sudden, unexpected leaping up during
> meditation in the art gallery during the visit
> by the Dalai Lama to bless the [sand] mandala.
> He had asked us to meditate for a brief period,
> and we did, a room filled with people,

including several monks. I had been attempting to purify myself by the *Dorje sempa* practice, I felt successful, then we went into the brief communal meditation, and I experienced this jump—no other way to explain it. A lift into the air, freedom, joy. It was short, a skip, and it made me want to write this book [What book? This one?] simply because it was so short and so unexpected and so cheerful.

The Dalai Lama had entered the room with two monks and some security people. One of them, a Tibetan, had come in before him, had examined the dais on which he was to sit, searched under its covering and examined the brightly coloured cushion. Then the Lama strolled in, stopped for a moment to look at prayer flags, examined a tanka hanging on a wall, listened to greetings, said a few words in thanks, smiled, meandered over to his cushion, and then chanted for two or three minutes. He suggested the meditation [during which the jump occurred] and afterwards chanted his short blessing. After finishing, he said cheerfully, breaking up the solemnity, "That's it," got up and strolled around the room, talking to people. . . .

What interests me now is that I had been too self-conscious to hold my hands in the appropriate mudra or to close my eyes, which I like to do while meditating. I thought this would look as if I was showing off. But why be self-conscious? The monks, the Lama, were not self-conscious. We are weighted down with expectations, others' views of us.

The account ends with a depressing reference to public opinion, illustrating the perhaps racial, certainly religious, intolerance in our society:

Pat Bovey, curator of the gallery, said that when, a couple of years earlier, the gallery had a ceremony dedicating a shinto shrine it was installing, people phoned constantly objecting. Some of the calls, from Christians, were so unpleasant, that she in turn phoned the Anglican bishop and the Catholic bishop, asking for advice. She told them she didn't know what to do. But the [sand] mandala construction and blessing invoked not one call. She said the monks appeared to have brought their own peace and gaiety with them.

Certainly the monks may have brought their own peace and gaiety with them, producing a packed wholeness, like that of an egg or an apple or a planet. However, equally, those who object to religious or cultural ceremonies and beliefs not their own, who fragment society with competitive political ambitions and national hatreds, are without intention sundering the whole.

Certain words stand out in these accounts: peace and gaiety

to do with the monks, and primarily "joy". Shelley, no matter what her temperament generally, was unexpectedly drenched in joy. I knew the brief spurt of joy, a tiny taste (which obviously had little effect because I forgot it), when its unexpected arrow shot through my body.

Of far more interest than this tiny flush is an episode somewhat similar to, but more explosive and detailed, than Shelley's: an exquisite description of joy given by Margaret Prescott Montague (1878–1955). Her book, *Twenty Minutes of Reality*, is unobtainable so I am using a quotation from *An Illustrated Encyclopedia of Mysticism*, edited by John Ferguson:

> [Montague] was recovering from an operation, and had been in a state of acute mental depression, having come to a sense that there was no God, or else an indifferent one. Her bed was wheeled out into the open. It was March; there was no trace of spring; but the wind blowing made an impact on her imagination. As she lay there, for the first time in her life she 'caught a glimpse of the ecstatic beauty of reality'. The experience was so overwhelming that she could not afterwards remember whether it was gradual or sudden. 'I saw no new thing, but I saw all the usual things in a miraculous new light—in what I believe is their true light. I saw for the first time how wildly beautiful and joyous, beyond any words of mine to describe, is the whole of life. Every human being moving across the porch, every

Rona Murray

sparrow that flew, every branch tossing in the wind, was caught in and was part of the whole mad ecstasy of loveliness, of joy, of importance, of intoxication of life.' A gleam of sunshine catching the hair of a nurse was a vision of eternal beauty, a sparrow chirping was one of the sons of God shouting for joy. The experience was one of falling in love with all around her.

This revelation changed Margaret Montague's life in that despite physical disabilities, including progressive blindness and later almost total deafness, she was able to say, "If the world be shut without, I'll sail the hidden seas within," and she communicated eloquently through books and articles. Others—many; I choose two—have become messengers of the quality of their experience: Whitman throughout *Leaves of Grass* in which every particle of mankind and cosmos is celebrated ("Joy, Joy. All over joy"), and Blaise Pascal who, at thirty-one according to Bucke, experienced a remarkable transcendence. He wrote a tumbled account which he stuffed into an amulet and always wore: "Joy, joy, joy, tears of joy. I do not separate myself from thee. They left me behind, me a fountain of living water. My God, do not leave me. Let me not be separated from thee. . . ."

Mankind universally desires joy, oneness, non-separation, purpose. Even the most pragmatic among us must at times yearn for something more than appears on the surface of existence;

the most evil in their sad sickness must at times glimpse their divorce from humanity and desire wholeness. In Job, it is the devil who walks up and down the earth and is aware of Man's frail grasp on non-separation, on how tempting it is for him to succumb to the negative. In *Paradise Lost* it is Satan, once Lucifer, brightest of all the angels, who suffers irretrievably, not because he is thrown out of a hierarchical heaven, but because he is divorced from God.

Not only mystics and religious celebrants gravitate toward wholeness. Some modern scientists, in particular proponents of the Gaia theory, stress our planet's harmonious self-regulating oneness, a cooperation we at times appear incapable of recognizing. I like an amusing analogy given by a friend in his explanation of mitochondria, cellular structures which, according to microbiologist Lynn Margulis, originated as bacteria that invaded cells: "foreigners who came to dinner and stayed." Before the advent of these guests, before the invasion of the mitochondria, my friend points out, life was not very interesting, nothing happened; there was an obvious need for this particular component that produces the necessary energy for whatever the cell wants to do. The happy cooperation between the guest and the cell's original organelles, which lacked their own energy, suggests that evolution occurred through cooperation, symbiotic relationships, as much as through the competition of natural selection.

It is we who do not always cooperate with the natural order, a self-regulating mechanism in which every action is countered with a reaction. It's possible to speculate a dramatic reaction would occur if we, as a component of non-cooperating life, crashed the system through limitless depletion of the ozone layer, a form of oxygen which filters out the sun's lethal ultraviolet rays.

God knows, the earth is doing her best to work towards harmonious resolutions. For example, the news at the moment is filled with wonder at the extraordinary behaviour of the lowly scented geranium (*Pelargonium* sp.), not noted for its somewhat indifferent flower, but for the lovely lemony fragrance of its leaves. Researchers at the University of Guelph have (naturally) applied for a patent on the plant since discovering it absorbs heavy metal and organic pollutants at an astonishing rate. Not only is it able to detoxify waste industrial areas, of which there are thousands, but also to thrive in the process and rapidly turn the salvaged earth into productive arable land.

In addition, the human population, which has spread like an uncontrolled cancer over the planet until balance is lost, is apparently now being controlled, not only through AIDS and famine, but also through a surprising drop in male sperm counts caused, scientists hazard, by industrial pollution:

> Is chemical pollution going to be the ultimate contraceptive? Is this the planet's secret self-defence mechanism against a species that got too smart for its own good, in its haste to consume the planet's rapidly diminishing resources? Studies that are currently under way will tell. It all goes to show how little we understand about what we are doing, on this glorious place called earth.[5]

Besides botanists and biologists, other researchers with open minds are considering the riddles and questions which bemuse us: what caused the universe and how did life begin? What is the meaning of evolutionary function and how does it work towards survival? Psychiatrist Anthony Stevens in *Private Myths* suggests dreams may be an evolutionary survival mechanism in that they work with symbols and restore *mysterium*—the recognition of the numinous—as a biological imperative that is crucial if we are to survive and heal a fragmented society:

> There needs to be a collective understanding
> that we are all part of one ecological whole
> and each of us is responsible for its sustenance:
> practically, to restore the primordial balance
> between our species and all other life on the
> planet. Instead of behaving like "hooligans" . . .
> we need to show some deference and humil-
> ity. Dreams, Stevens says, "are our last
> wilderness, to be protected with the same
> fervour as the rain forest, the only natural oa-
> sis of spiritual vitality left to us."[6]

Gregg Easterbrook, in the science section of the *Globe and Mail* (24 October 1998) quotes Alfred Russel Wallace, co-discoverer with Darwin of the evolutionary theory of natural selection, who spoke of "the unseen universe of spirit." Easterbrook, in his essay originally titled "Beside Still Waters: Searching for Meaning in an Age of Doubt," dismisses the postmodernist philosophy of life as recognizing no more than

Rona Murray

a "chance manifestation of pitiless mechanical forces," and in its place posits: "New findings in science point toward a buoyant view of our being, one in which life is favoured, not improbable, and the universe a welcoming place, not an obdurate domain." He speaks of religious leaders (including the Pope) taking steps toward accepting evolutionary biology as profoundly elegant, and scientists, with the Big Bang theory proving more and more acceptable, considering the "splendid powers at the core of existence."

Possibly—at least from an excited observer's point of view—scientific speculation, metaphysical positives, and psychiatric explorations appear to be drawing closer together, with biologists and physicists exploring the territory of mystics and poets, the territory of Rumi, Rilke, and Hopkins; Whitman, Plotinus, Buddha, and Jesus. In any case, many thoughtful watchers agree we have for one reason or other been schooled to view our existence as competitive and fragmented, and it is now time to shift our sights, to recognize and celebrate our wholeness, our place in a magnificent cosmology, a welcoming, buoyant, and joyful universe:

> I celebrate
> the body of the earth
> each particle
> > particular and absolute
> grain
> > flake
> > > eye bright or dying
> each hair
> > of every feather
> > > of every wing

geometry of agate
mysterious as seas
where grasses undulate and make
cloudy transparencies

               filamented moths' wings
skeletal leaves
          snow falling
tentacles of ice
          hoar frost on
barb and stem
          winter solstice
silence

I celebrate
bulb beneath the sod
egg within the goose
sun burning

all craft

this house
worms' hieroglyphs upon the centre post
cedar limbs holding up the roof
stars moon madrigals
mountain light

I celebrate
the soft nose of the horse
tongue licking
creamy whiteness of the duck
where the wings join at his back
the gay flicker
that housels in the eaves all winter

I celebrate
our dance   our dying
your body
each upstanding hair   follicle   cuticle   freckle
the blood
          in our veins

the turning over of the heart
the insistent ticking of the clock

the making.

$\mathcal{P}$OSSIBILITY

AFTER MY FIRST ATTEMPT AT THIS BOOK, in which I used almost entirely other people's poetry in trying to express what I wanted to say, my editor told me I should use my own, some of which had been written years before but was, she said, in touch with the space I was after. I reread it, and yes, some of it fits in meaningfully. Possibly the following poem, entitled "Homing"—intended literally and concerned with the exhilaration I felt on returning after a long absence to the part of the country in which I had once lived—could equally well be about our true homing:

> Come clear now:
>> the circle is arcing
>> round to its start
>>> the pinpoint origin
>>> about to be met
>>>> a coming back
>>>> from the going forth

doors and windows now thrown wide
that sea-salt may impregnate
sill   stairwell   upper room

vigilant ghosts
be exorcised

[You out there
do you recognize
your journey
        beginning
        middle
        drawing in
                Tides
                winds
                shale and shell
                        detritus
                        holding?]

                Granite   pale grass   arbutus skin
                    move into my poem
                    into my knowing plexus
                                core
                                caw
                                cry of self

                The recognition must
                take count of every particle

            the reach be into
          four multiplied by four
              by four again
                directions

        the grasp be for all
          scraps whirling
      up down between across

                  twisting papers
                  fragmented words
                  images found/lost
                  old loves   hates
                      bones broken beneath
                      elephant feet

          All   all immersed
          in hot sun acrid cow-parsley
          wild rose   broom
          iodine kelp salt
                earth dear cedar bough
                      after rain

Steady steady
on the sheet:
          hand shakes to record
          (long stilled tears threaten release)
                    exile return
                    circle complete

to record promise given
not understood:

a private vision
of brand burned which should
select for the swinging arc/k
a sliver of flesh and bone

thrown out
alone

Longing
draws bird fish and beast
draws petal to dust
insect into
metamorphosis

draws the sick soul
or the sainted
draws all   at last

home

[Do you recollect
do *you* recollect
those places
where you drowned
in the dark
testing the current
to see if

                    frail will
            could last?]

Old sailors cried
        on sighting black toothed shores
                        —Have mercy   Lord
                            upon our souls—

                        I cry
                        [you cry   *cry*]
                            mercy

Let me count
        slow stones
        sucked by tide
        watch
        bees with pollen packs
        on swollen legs
        burrow into poppy heads
                so weighted over
                with dark seed
                they droop towards
                    homing earth

                    Freighted/naked
                        even
                        so

I wrote "Homing" after going through and emerging from the period of painful upheaval ("Midway on our life's journey, I found myself/ In dark woods, the right road lost"[7]), emotional and financial, which often attacks, or perhaps illuminates, those entering the middle portion of their lives. I am glad I wrote it, if only because now it recalls the passion I felt at the time: the need to recognize and recall the larger moments (eons?) we live through, just as I feel challenged and committed to remembering that other, seemingly more truthful, state I experienced during the gravel pit accident. A part of me (a kind of Ancient Mariner part, collaring impatient people who have more important things to do) insists I let others know they are not alone in their suffering, isolation, betrayal, or in their crazy, unexpected exaltation.

That need returns me to the planet as we know it and to the extraordinary paradigm shift regarding our world and its cosmos which is taking place in scientific conjecture at this moment. This shift towards considering the earth and all it contains as a living, intelligent organism rather than a purposeless machine mirrors the "knowing" of a blissful, loving universe with which I and so many others have had a serendipitous encounter.

A "profound transformation . . . in the way scientists view their world," a shift in their framework of thought is taking place. Paul Davies and John Gribbin, proponents of the New Science, state: "From time to time in the history of ideas, a shift occurs in the basic paradigm. When this happens, not only do scientific theories change, but the scientists' conception of the world changes as well. That is what is happening now."

If we could keep this shift, the findings of the New Science, quantum mechanics, in our minds while regarding our surroundings, we should possibly visualize everything we see, touch, and feel as connected and shot through with light: living, sparking, the reverse of the formless and inert. Artist Andy Lakey saw the cosmos in this way during his near death due to overdosing on drugs. He remembered the images and after recovery painted canvas after canvas depicting his "angels": odd, glowing entities with no resemblance to our romantic medieval portrayals:

> I felt a twirling sensation, like a little tornado or whirlpool around my feet. I didn't see them in detail, but I knew there were seven figures, and as they twirled up toward my knees, my thighs, my waist and up to my chest, the twirl-ing got faster and faster. It was like a whirlwind, but I was standing still, and I saw the water splattering around me [in the shower]. When they reached my heart, they came together as one and put their arms around me, or maybe I should say its arms around me, because now there was only one figure—exactly like the figures you see in my paintings. It had a ta-pered body with stublike arms, and a featureless head elevated above the body. It put its arms around me and I felt a wonderful, warm rush of unconditional love as it lifted me into another dimension. There were a thou-sand planets with ten thousand poles of light

extending through them and into the void. Every pole and planet interacted with the others; every pole pierced other poles and planets, like a galaxy of brightness in cellophane and iridescent colours. . . .

"Every pole and planet interacted with the others; every pole pierced other poles and planets, like a galaxy of brightness. . . ." This is not, of course, how any of us sees the cosmos, but it does appear to reflect some of the hypothetical findings of quantum physicists in that their universe is a form of electromagnetic energy which operates through connections. However, although we are not, as far as our senses tell us, in that stunning, non-material universe, and although we may fervently love our earth, drawing our fingers over the solid, satisfying textures of wood and stone and silk, we still experience unlocalized loss which may be identified as separation, lack of connection.

On some days I find the passion, carrying with it an inexplicable melancholy, for our exquisite planet and all it contains overwhelming. Today, for example, I watched four otters playing a kind of tag with each other close to the shore at low tide. One of them climbed onto a rock which is generally submerged and sat there with something, seaweed or fish, hanging from its mouth, when a bald eagle flew at it, trying to snatch away this meal and failing. I had never before seen an eagle so close and was stunned by its size and beauty—brilliant white against night-dark feathers. Meantime, seals lie on rocky islands throughout the bay, Canada geese in their immaculately patterned outer garments (who dreamed up these creatures, this diversity?) forage along the shore guarding their week-old goslings, oystercatchers and kingfishers swoop, screaming idiosyncratic clicks and cries, over the sea. The melancholy may be anxiety. The goslings may not all be there; the seals appear to be whelping too early, particularly since it has been such a cold spring. But it isn't that. The melancholy is not attached to anything; it's free floating. It has to do with loss.

I realize it is easy for me to respond to the earth in this way—a way all of us, or at least many of us, feel at one time or another—because of where I live. However, the response is not idiosyncratic but a part of our natures, although perhaps it is more marked, or available, if one inhabits a low-human-density segment of the earth close to wild creatures.

I am talking about the west coast of Canada, in particular Metchosin, a Salish word meaning "stinking fish", referring either to a dead whale which once rotted on the beach or to the area in which the Kakyaakun tribe extracted oil from herring. This is a rural community on the southern tip of Vancouver Island, along the shore of the Pacific Ocean, formerly covered with Douglas fir, hemlock, cedar (once used by native peoples for dugout canoes, totems, longhouses, cooking utensils, garments), Sitka spruce, maple, salal, and Oregon grape. North of where I am, on the Queen Charlotte Islands for example, the rainfall is exceedingly heavy, but on the southern tip of our island it is moderate, the same as much of Europe.

The day my accident occurred, the sea in front of our windows had a distant white scarf of fog lying on it. The weather had been wet and foggy so we hadn't, for weeks, seen the Olympic Mountains across the Juan de Fuca Strait and the border with the United States. These mountains, snow tipped even in the summer, constantly change colour, sometimes pale blue, sometimes deep, sometimes clear purple, and may be outlined so crisply against the sky they could be cut-out stage scenery. A bank of mist often travels down the strait for long distances between our two countries. Then from our side, it appears as if Port Angeles, forty miles away, is wrapped in a grey blanket and from its side we must seem mysteriously dangerous with our foghorn crying out painfully, but we're actually both in bright sunlight. While I write this, I realize for the first time why the cleft in the mountains is called "The Angels' Gap". Of course, because the port of the angels is there, actually a small, unimaginative town, but filled with promise at night when its lights gleam out of the darkness.

A point of land far to our right holds, ironically, a prison and another to our left a military camp. Islands in our bay are rich with mussels, their clinging strands tangled with tiny snails, their purple shells anchored with baby barnacles; they can be six inches long with flesh bright orange when cooked. Delicious, they are not generally eaten because people don't know they are there, or if they know believe they are not edible. No doubt as sea life becomes even more diminished (there's almost no salmon here now, few oysters or clams), harvesters will discover them, and they'll be gone.

Just offshore, a few small islands with names (most are unnamed) are called the Haystocks. They look like haystacks and also like ancient European barrows. When we first came here, I was curious about them: how could rock islands, by nature bare or with a scattering of earth, barely enough for

Rona Murray

wildflowers, bunch up into symmetrical hard mounds twenty and thirty feet high? It took some time (no one seemed to have answers) to ascertain they were probably Aboriginal burial grounds, possibly used as death chambers when smallpox ravaged the tribes who lived nearby and fished the plentiful ocean. The living placed the dead in canoes, piled the earth into more canoes, paddled through the sea, and built layers of loam and corpses into large mounds where seabirds— cormorants and herons and oystercatchers and Canada geese and multiple varieties of ducks and gulls—gather. Some of those islands have hidden beaches of fragmented white shell where gulls dashed clams against the rocks to extract tender flesh. One has a navigational marker. Often an eagle perches on it.

Migrating sea lions pass through our strait and stay for a time. They may come up, three or four, one after the other, from beneath your canoe. They appear to be single-minded; unlike seals who nose around curiously but like athletes using the Australian crawl, they refuse to be sidetracked. Their heads are the size of mammoth beach balls. You may find the skin creeps across your back, gives a shudder, but they will not be interested in you.

Seals congregate on the islands, the close ones and the more distant: hundreds of them—so many, the fishermen want to kill them. At the moment they are protected. On sunny days they lie on the rocks as close together as human sunbathers in photographs of Hawaii and the Mediterranean. Their fronts gleam silver in the sun, but their backs are dark so when they balance on small rocks with their tails and heads up in the air, they look like fat wooden rockers attached to children's play horses. Their large round eyes are calm and friendly. One wants to pet them. Their pups are generally not born until about the middle of July and every year I go through various stages of despair, wondering why they haven't done it yet. Also, before the birthing they disappear for at least a month, and I worry that they've been poisoned by pollution, or the fishers finally have permission to kill them, or they have decided to migrate elsewhere. But then they come back, mothers give birth and afterwards go off to feed, sometimes for up to twenty-four hours:

> July ends: apples drop onto parched grass,
> blackberries' garnet blood stains the teeth,
> and butter yellow goslings are flown or lost.
>
> Seals whelp beyond the garden: their progeny,
> small as human newborns, lie on juts of cliff
> and island rocks, sticky from their birth, flippers
> impotently crossed. Their necks turn and stretch
> as the canoe approaches, denying our fear they
> are stillborn corpses.
>
> Their mothers are off hunting. Those that
> have come back hump on land or swim between
> strangers and their pups; marbled heads
> rear up, eyes alert and questioning. Cool
> flippers nudge their young, stroke up on up,
> indicating where their paps, ripe with milk, wait
> for suck, or nudge them down for that first plunge
> into their natural habitat.

They swim in pairs, a large head by a smaller,
or mothers carry young, lacing weightless through
the green, translucent, salty element, twisting
heads at times to nuzzle pups upon
their backs.

They dive, skim purple starfish, anemones' thin
fronds pulsing back and forth, slide through drifts
of kelp, over mussel shells, humped indigo,
and barnacles sharp as splintered bone
gripping rocks.

> Quiet. Quiet.
> Our sundered lives
> reshape themselves.

Possibly the melancholy we experience is born less from
fear of loss than from deep-rooted knowledge of being sundered
from the natural world. I want to recognize and take mindful
notice when walking over sand or stones on the beach, over
solidified lava, seaweed that pops when you tread on it, over
tiny shells and bits of flotsam, twenty-foot ropes of kelp with
dark ribbons attached to the bulbs. Underwater, the ribbons
become long hair—floating free, undulating gently—of
drowned women. Above the beach, snowberry, broom, reddish
salal, wild roses, Oregon grape with cloudy blue berries, and
scarlet-skinned arbutus hold up the bank. In spring, purple
shooting stars, white Easter lilies, blue camas, chocolate lilies,
trilliums, pink sedum, and minute spreading flowers and mosses
carpet earth over rock. The scent is chiefly of cedar and Douglas

fir. A warm fragrance comes from the leaves, not flowers, of wild roses.

The Salish people collected the camas bulbs—their potato—as a rich source of food. The vivid flower has yellow pollen–laden anthers. Christians say the trillium represents the trinity because it has three of everything—leaves, sepals, petals—but it was here long before the Christians.

Seabirds don't sing; they cry out with high-pitched, dripping voices, make harsh, clacking noises like the kingfisher or rough, squawking cries like the heron as it goes home to its tree at five o'clock after a day of silent fishing. The dark oystercatchers with red eyes and beaks scream if anything approaches their nests, and the Canada geese, sometimes in a V, sometimes in pairs, whirr over the water, honking. Swans, mute, occasionally visit, swimming ashore and walking ungainly on the beach.

I think of one of the Blessings, all of which acknowledge love, diversity, and plenty, in the Hebrew wedding ceremony: "Blessings of white space—of spontaneity, surprise, and joy— of possibility in a universe that is better to us than we would ever have thought to be to ourselves."

Richness and plenty must be acknowledged. In the medieval world it was a romantic dream of Cockayne—where grapes, already wine, bent themselves down to fill the sensuous mouth—rather than a possibility. Here it is often a reality:

Blackberries

fat on the tongue
burst purple
under an August sun

my nails
stained black
hour after hour pick
wine and winter jam
but these berries are so profligate
I cannot catch
their pulpy fruit
before its weight
pulls vines to earth
and spills in inky
waste

Peaches
—little golden suicides—
fall from the west wall
break
gentleness
on tarmac
Apples
lie in grass
until their pith
is eaten out
and empty balls of tissued skin
tease wasps
too full to sting

It is too much
Cockayne is here
and all day long
I try to force some order on
a universe
so absurdly generous
it stuns
the small and dubious
human mind.

The New Science, based on the quantum theory of physics rather than on the seventeenth-century mechanical clock world devised by Newton, suggests we have made our mistake in assuming we can force the order I apparently desired in this poem on a universe which is by its nature tumbling, changing, transforming: the reverse of the predictable mechanistic structure we have been taught to expect. It is also the reverse of the "common sense" we have devised in order to account for a world viewed as immutable in time and space, length and mass, all of which, according to mathematicians, are relative, dependent on our particular perspective. To simplify, we all know our eyes actually see the physical world upside down and our mind comfortably transforms it to right side up (for us) because that suits us better: "The effect of observation is absolutely fundamental to the reality that is revealed" (Davies and Gribbin), and that (revealed) reality is not necessarily the one with which we actually live.

In this new paradigm, our environment is such that we need to be open to endless possibilities and connections since matter (everything we regard as physical) consists of relationships and the energy they generate in forming a holistic, indeterminate, and open system in an interlocking whole. If we return to Chet Raymo's ecstatic description of the universe, it's easy to swim into his evocation of a constantly mutating fluid cosmos, constructed more like fire or water than our concept of physical solidity.

On the other hand, if we look at the orderly, predictable way in which the natural world, until we fiddle with it, is organized, we see a different and accepted reality. Animals, including humans, rarely breed across species; the seasons follow each other in an orderly progression, night follows day, every living creature is born, needs sustenance, has the urge to procreate, and dies. We know what to expect, but according to the New Science only within probabilities: there is no absolute because contained in a general order there is the unpredictability of choice at all levels. There is no inert, passive matter shaped and formed by external forces as Newton postulated, no living creatures who are little more than "gene machines"; instead the New Science suggests a cosmos of finely tuned, far less substantial matter, radiant with sparks of energy producing a cosmic network of information, ideas, and self-organizing connections.

This shift returns us to Aristotle, who viewed the universe as a magnificent organism directed toward a final, mysterious goal: a concept, according to scientists Davies and Gribbin, away from reductionism and toward holism.

The universe of the quantum physicists is held in place by fields: invisible, non-material structures, which operate in space. Space is no longer empty with vast distances between the particles and electrons in the atoms of our bodies as well as between the heavenly bodies in galaxies, but is filled with gravitational fields, electromagnetic fields, quantum fields, possibly morphogenic fields—all media of connection. Regarding morphogenic fields, Margaret Wheatley (*Leadership and the New Science*) points out that "after part of the species has learned a behaviour, such as bicycle riding, others will find it easier to learn that skill." Biologists who observe animals suggest similar dispersed learning. Many times scientists, inventors, musicians have arrived simultaneously at hypotheses, inventions, notations: on occasion, court cases have resulted. Alternatively, of course, creative individuals may have been ready to make the same discoveries at the same time. Even so, physical reactions may also suggest unseen connections: I doubt if I am alone in finding my legs and feet, rooted to the ground, set up a wild tingling if I see somebody, especially a child, too near the edge of a cliff. Pain and passion transfer from victim to reader or viewer, one reason certain books and movies are so successful: are we so vicarious, such voyeurs, because everything that happens, happens, in a sense, to us?

As a further medium of connection, "empty" space is now filled with electronic networks of voices, music, advertising, drama, messages carried on limitless informative airwaves. Our globe is shrinking; we are growing closer to each other every day.

The New Scientists assert this cosmos is constantly changing, inventing and renewing itself, existing through relationships ranging from those between minute, unseen particles in all matter to those in galaxies far beyond the reach of our telescopes. They claim to have produced experimental evidence that elementary particles are "affected by connections that exist unseen across time and space" (Wheatley). These connections remain, apparently, no matter how far each one travels. In this structure, nothing is separate so we, members of mankind, cannot stand back, observe, and make judgements as we have done in the past when we presumed to be in some way separate from and more intelligent than everything else. Instead of being a lordly element in a mechanical structure, invented long ago and operating in cool isolation, we are constantly creating our reality. We cannot, in this new frame of reference, observe without affecting the observed: observer and observed are inextricably and intimately interwoven because we are part of each other; we are the same thing. Early on in this new way of thinking, astronomer James Jeans suggested the universe was beginning to look more like a great thought than a great machine.

❧

At this point, I have to get up and fetch myself a glass of wine. As I type "we are constantly creating our reality" it is inevitable that the mind which produces the thought flashes onto this century with all its brutality; its *second* thought hovers on the exquisite world we live in and which presumably, following this reasoning, we have also created. Then the mind points out this hypothesis is close to Hindu, and other, mysticism; after that it ruminates on the possibility that the quantum physics' cosmology is in keeping with the beliefs of Christian Scientists. About that, I am ambiguous, having felt in the past arrogantly contemptuous toward what appeared to me an unsympathetic and self-serving philosophy. Comforting myself, I remember Mary Baker Eddy was strongly influenced by Eastern thought.

Finally, I recall my accident: the calmness, bliss, "at homeness" of being a consciousness held in the womb of the energy-driven dance of the universe. No longer separate. This experience, more and more usual, relates, it seems to me, to the shift in scientific thinking which reasons we are all, everything, part of a pulsing, radiant whole. Perhaps it also stands in contradistinction to the ills of anomie, disengagement, barrenness, loneliness (leading in some cases to suicide and obscene violence) driving much of our more and more acquisitive Western society today.

The cosmos of the New Science does not begin to give us all the answers we desire. In the past, we have set up a world of boundaries which provided us with a corral of safety, an illusion of knowing and predictability. We have lived and do live in a technically brilliant society and behave like gods in our attempts to create life itself. Even so, physicists studying the structure of the universe are aware of how limited in real knowledge we are: "One learns to hope that nature possesses an order that one may aspire to comprehend" (C. M. Yang in Wheatley).

Gary Zukav, exploring the new physics in *The Dancing Wu Li Masters*, points out, "The whole corpus of classical physics and the technology that rests on it is about the separateness of things, about constituent parts and how they influence each other across their separateness." He describes that mechanical and anti-human world: "Classical physics transmuted the living cosmos of Greek and medieval times, a cosmos filled with purpose and intelligence and driven by the love of God for the benefit of humans, into a dead, clockwork machine; cold silence pervaded the once teeming heavens. Human beings and their struggles, the whole of consciousness, and life itself were

Rona Murray

irrelevant to the workings of the vast universal machine."

In that machine universe, according to modern physicists, creation works in an automatic, almost somnambulant manner, with each part of it, isolated wheels and cogs, chugging along until the predictable end arrives and it winds down to a stop. Margaret J. Wheatley: "Loneliness pervaded not only our science, but whole cultures. In America, we raised individualism to its highest expression, each of us protecting our boundaries, asserting our rights, creating a culture [of isolation]."

In protecting our boundaries and in our desire for order, we have formed nation-states, governments, defence departments, police, food distribution centres, communities and welfare organizations, education and health structures, business conglomerates (positive and negative), multinational corporations, technical and scientific laboratories. All these endeavours are "joinings" of individual interests, and, if not all, most are built on self-interest. At the same time, in Western civilization, we tend to live as self-centred individuals in nuclear families and gated communities, having lost the knowledge of completeness, of being lively parts of the whole. No matter how many friends we may have, how many family members, how many successes, we are surrounded, if only occasionally aware of our emptiness, by an aura of isolation and loss.

Our literature and art, our theatre, our classical music with its clicks and spins, all express breakdown and alienation. In advertising and the media, we promote formulaic beauty leading to the objectification of people, particularly of women, with multiple images of hair, teeth, long legs, and tight buttocks often divorced from the whole person. Equally, our magazines and screens are rampant with the lure of material acquisition and mechanical sex, substituting the erotic for love: but the erotic does not give us that melding into the other or into the universe which is the core of love; its pleasure is temporary, self-seeking, and, with meagre thought for the other, stimulates endless hunger for further experimentation.

I wrote the small poem above, "Blackberries", with its paltry need for order over a sumptuous universe, long before hearing of the New Science, almost all of which is still a mystery to me, as it is, I expect, to most people. However, an introduction to its theories has provided an opportunity to look in a new way at what had previously appeared to me as chance rather than energy-generating connection. Was that car accident chance? Perhaps probability. At least it generated intellectual energy. Now I try to think in terms of synergy. This method approaches Jung's concept of synchronicity ("meaningful coincidence of outer and inner events that are not themselves causally connected") and consists in observing how new energy is generated through apparently random relationships; and how, far from being distinct entities, we are part of a universe which exists through connectedness. According to this view, we are, along with everything else, the sinews of a whole constantly reinventing itself by liberating streams of energy and engaging in a great dance mythologized long ago as that of Shiva creating and destroying as he invents and tramples the cosmos:

> Subatomic particles forever partake of this
> unceasing dance of annihilation and creation.
> In fact, subatomic particles *are* this unceasing
> dance of annihilation and creation. This twen-
> tieth-century discovery, with all its psychedelic

implications, is not a new concept. In fact, it is very similar to the way that much of the earth's population, including the Hindus and the Buddhists, view their reality.

Hindu mythology is virtually a large-scale projection into the psychological realm of microscopic scientific discoveries. Hindu deities such as Shiva and Vishnu continually dance the creation and destruction of universes while the Buddha image of the wheel of life symbolizes the unending process of birth, death, and rebirth which is a part of the world of form, which is emptiness, which is form. (Zukav)

Some quantum physicists play with the possibility of interlocking, parallel universes, and claim nothing is lost. All the potentials are retained, waiting exploration. If we choose to take one road, "the one less travelled by," or to make a life-altering choice, is the other road, the other possibility, still there? If we are "out of our bodies" are we in another timespace universe? One, apparently, that is gentler than our own. It sounds like the wildest kind of science fiction. Perhaps it is.

In any case, this new "reality" connects with the territory of Yeats' *Spiritus Mundi* and Jung's collective unconscious as well as the hypothetical kingdoms, already considered, of lovers and mystics.

Of course, the New Science is new science; its mathematics and experimentations may be faulty and its theories as stunningly impossible as they appear to be. Some mathematicians regard much of its territory as nonsense. Even so, occasionally we may—through accident, drug, dance, love, illness, meditation—sunder the skin of the mechanistic world in which we have imprisoned ourselves and experience something else.

No one knows what the universe is about. We postulate what we prefer to believe. Faust needlessly sold his soul to the devil for further knowledge. Possibly the best we can do is shake off some of our preconceptions, look about us with open eyes, and be happy, because those who are happy at least do no harm. An ancient Chinese proverb tells us: "The bird does not sing because he has an answer; he sings because he has a song."

CONNECTION

Sad hunter
why do you row
so passionately down
the length of the lake?

Is it the wild goose
circling overhead
crying a child's heart-break
that galvanizes
your jerky muscles
into this mad race?

Or is it his mate
bloodied
in the bottom of your boat
whose dead eyes mock
your failing strength?

THIS INCIDENT WAS TOLD TO ME BY THE HUNTER, who said geese mate for life and remain without a partner if one of them dies. I think this has been disproved, but he believed it and was unnerved when, after killing a female, the male followed him, crying out, until he finally reached a far shore. He never hunted wildfowl again.

That is a small, straightforward connection between a pair of geese and between a man and two geese. There are many far more mysterious connections between animals and between animals and peoples. The North American West Coast whalers, for example, used to go through rigorous cleansing and spiritual training before the hunt. I was told of the case, taking place at the time within living memory, of a chief whaler whose dream spirit was able to leave his body and communicate with a whale, urging it to "find" the hunter's shaft; once it was brought to shore, the women danced, paid homage to the great animal by scattering it with blue ducks' feathers and eagle down, and then shared the meat with the tribe. Unfortunately, this particular whaler fell into a trance of some kind, possibly connected with his spirit callings, and was believed to be dead. The men of the tribe broke his legs, a usual procedure, so he could fit into a burial box which was to be anchored high in the trees. The pain roused him abruptly; men and women at the ceremony, terrified, believed he was a ghost and ran away, leaving him destitute for decades to crawl along the beach hunting for food and water until he finally died.

This story appears improbable but its spirit- or dream-calling claim is backed by a fascinating account from Arthur Grimble, a British administrator for many years in the Gilbert Islands, who wrote *A Pattern of Islands* (1952). Apparently, he was a particularly thin man and the islanders, believing a chief should be "fleshy from head to foot," told him he should eat porpoise flesh as then he would swell in the proper places. They offered to take him by canoe to Kuma, where the High Chief's hereditary porpoise-caller operated. Once they arrived, the caller said he would go into his dream world and have the great mammals there between three and four o'clock: "Wait in peace now. I go on my journey."

Four o'clock passed. Grimble says he was thoroughly skeptical and growing impatient, when a "strangled howl burst from the dreamer's hut. I jumped round to see his cumbrous body come hurtling head first through the torn screen. . . . Then words came gulping out of him: 'They come, they come! Our friends from the west. . . . Let us go down and greet them.'"

Garlands had been woven and the makings of a feast prepared. The islanders and Grimble rushed into the sea; the porpoises gambolled "towards us at a fine clip" and then apparently disappeared.

> In the strained silence that followed, I thought they were gone. The disappointment was so sharp, I did not stop to think then that, even so, I had seen a very strange thing. I was in the act of touching the dreamer's shoulder to take my leave when he turned his still face to me: "The king of the west comes to meet me," he murmured, pointing downwards. My eyes followed his hand. There, not ten yards away, was the great shape of a porpoise poised like a glimmering shadow in the glass-green

water. Behind it followed a whole dusky flotilla of them.

They were moving towards us in extended order with spaces of two or three yards between them, as far as my eye could reach. So slowly they came they seemed to be hung in a trance.

The villagers welcomed the porpoises ashore; the women and children herded them from behind, clapping softly and singing. Their guests, grounded against the sand, were lifted and garlanded while the natives burst into a frenzy of noise and excitement. The porpoises, who seemed oddly hypnotized, were carved up; some were eaten, some salted and kept for the future. Arthur Grimble says he was so upset by the slaughter, he was quite unable to eat the prize pieces put aside for him.

Years ago, in the late sixties, I lived for a time outside the small town of Castlegar, in the Kootenays, an exquisite and interesting part of British Columbia, where, towards the beginning of this century, the Doukhobors, an agrarian, unorthodox religious order of people, had settled. At the beginning of the century, they had fled from Russia where they were persecuted for their recalcitrant (according to the authorities) attitudes towards religion, war, bureaucracy, and their children's education. Their creed was to live together communally and work with the earth. Pacifists, they believed that if you killed, you killed Christ in the other.

Walter, whom I met there, taught at an arts' school in Nelson, some distance away. Once we decided to live together in an area between our jobs, we bought an old Doukhobor farm, ten isolated acres above the Kootenay River, and started building a house as a communal enterprise. We also started living intimately, if inadvertently, with animals. Cedar waxwings and bears devoured our ancient apples when they turned to cider, becoming delightfully drunk. Mountain bluebirds produced so many young these brilliant creatures—at first glance appearing to be escaped budgies—occupied falling fence posts in every direction. Hairy woodpeckers knocked holes in the original house, and swallows nested with us in its decayed woodwork. Porcupines trundled through the knapweed acres; terrified stray cats appeared and with some coaxing stayed; a tiny, green, vociferous tree frog commandeered one of the steps in our new half-built house; two bitches, both far too young, impregnated at the same time by Troy, a long-haired German shepherd, produced over a dozen puppies. Our chickens manufactured orange-yolked eggs and our geese laid stillborn shells (this probably isn't possible. In any case, they nursed these oval disasters for weeks); clicking beetles infested our meagre bathroom: they reminded me of Kafka—I never killed them, although once in desperation while sitting on the toilet I flicked one off my naked leg and it landed, imperviously, with a sharp retort against the wall; butterflies flaked out of the sky; white-tailed deer deigned occasionally to dine on our disastrously dried-up pasture: there was little water but enough, with care, to dampen the marijuana plants a student or a son had planted. Walter and I stopped teaching briefly and lived on lamb's quarters while I wrote an unpublished novel and he made tiles for the new house and *raku* pots for fun.

The point of this lengthy introduction (I bet you wondered if there would ever be a point) is that I want to remember connections with a horse called by a plebeian name, Shane.

As a child, I had grown up with horses, loved them, and moving towards fifty, advanced for this kind of adolescent passion, wanted to ride again. I had heard a new community college was established somewhere in the interior of B.C., and, without careful thought, assumed that must be the Cariboo where I'd spent summers and knew the riding was largely through sage and grass with limitless unfenced acres to canter through. I applied for the job.

The Kootenay region was mountainous and forested, possible if not perfect riding country. Quite without money at the time, I found, in a junk store, an English saddle. It was decrepit, the seat torn from the tree, but was an optimistic symbol: if I had a saddle, I would get a horse.

Having been told weather in the Kootenays was much like that on the coast with its meagre January sleet, I was astonished, during my first winter in Castlegar, at the impenetrable five or six feet (compressed from fifteen) of snow. Two years later, on our "farm", we had to ski from our old Doukhobor house to the one we were building half a dozen acres away. An isolated family lived half a mile below us, and a chestnut gelding, ridden briefly perhaps a couple of times a year, lived with them. During the winter, he was enclosed in a circle roughly the size of an average living room bounded by high snowbanks.

Every day he trampled out his lonely territory. I started visiting him with a carrot or an apple when I walked down to fetch the mail. He nickered when he saw me. Horses are herd animals; they need companionship. Eventually I learned that Shane, an Anglo-Arab, had been imported from the States as a stud and had later been cruelly gelded: roped, thrown viciously to the ground, and left immobile for hours after the cutting. Since that time, he was not a dependable ride.

His owner had to move and offered him to me for what he had paid—an inconsiderable amount. I bought a bit and bridle, a halter, saddle blanket, hay, oats, salves for eyes and hooves, then oiled my English saddle and walked him up the steep hill to home.

Shane bucked me off twice within fifteen minutes. I had been taught by my father that before being a good rider one had to fall off a hundred times. I thought I had completed that number. He had also insisted that as soon as I fell off, I got on again. I did the first time, but the second, mercifully, Shane broke one of two girth straps and the saddle slipped under his belly. For the time being, I had to give up.

I did finally ride Shane but never with my old confidence, and for his companionship and ours we acquired a second horse, Classy. They became inseparable, sticking their heads in through the open window of our bedroom in the mornings when daylight arrived, grazing together, neighing wildly if one was taken out and not the other. They would race to us when we called them after returning from work. One day they didn't come and when we walked over the pastures, we found Classy tangled in fallen wire with Shane solidly by him, refusing to move until we had stripped off the barbs and twine.

When we left the Kootenays a couple of years later, we moved to five acres near Vancouver, taking horses and dogs with us. Classy could lift gate latches, no matter how securely we thought we had locked them; Shane, being smaller, could squirm into areas Classy couldn't and drag food out to share with him; they both escaped altogether too often in an urban neighbourhood, aiding each other in all adventures. I've been wondering (hopefully and sadly), after reading possibly too much about the New Physics, animals, and plants, if they kept in touch with each other in a mind way after they were separated when we moved, again, to Vancouver Island.

This time, we had no pasture and sold them for a small amount, providing they stayed together, to neighbours. Later, Shane was sold again and moved from one place to another. I didn't want to see him. More than riding, I had loved to groom him, clean out his hooves, feed him oil from a spoon, which he licked clean, bathe and anoint his eyes when flies settled on them, and above all to hear his excited nickers greeting me when I went looking for him.

One day I heard his new owners were not riding him; they were nervous, were thinking of moving, and were going to have him sold for foxmeat or pet food. I struggled with plans to turn our decrepit garage into a loose box, obtain rental pasture, and then went to talk to them. I found a young woman, not overly friendly—perhaps she had paid handsomely for him—and not in love with Shane but, even so, unwilling to destroy him. A neighbour was to take him as a companion for her donkey. I asked if I could see him, and the woman said of course, but he wouldn't come to anyone unless tempted with carrots. She gave me a couple, which I hid behind my back while walking out to the long pasture and calling his name. Shane threw his head up, listened, neighed his short, excited nickers, and then galloped up to me, nuzzling his nose into my neck. We were not sundered, despite being apart for over fifteen years, but he had been more loyal than I had, just as Rosemary, Malcolm Lowry's "meek and impossible" elephant, trumpeted at their coming together after long separation.

Walter and I never thought of ourselves as being part of an extended menagerie when we lived in the Kootenays, but, looking back, we were. We didn't bond with chickens, geese, or the birds with which we were sharing our tiny first house, but we did bond with Troy, a fiercely loyal German shepherd, given to me, unknowing, as a young dog, because he had bitten people. At parties, when I first met Walter, Troy, shoving between us, would let him but no one else dance with me. Workmen building our new house were terrified to move our car when we were not around, but when Troy and our other dogs returned one night looking like walruses after an encounter with a porcupine, he lay bleeding on the floor, licking my hand while I tried to extract barbed quills from his tongue, gums, and throat. He knew we were trying to help him, just as he knew, without any indication, that one of us was thinking of feeding him, taking him for a walk or ride.

Our present dog, a Bouvier, is also a mind reader like all the dogs and cats we've known. We understand her language: varying barks/half barks or small moans to go out, come in to a certain room, be invited onto the bed in the morning. We have not taught her to come and thank us for her supper, but she does, with a small lick or nose poked into a palm. Sharma has another interesting characteristic. In the mornings, when she first gets up, she sits immobile looking at the view out of the window. Later, she goes outside and, moving to the edge of the lawn, does the same thing. At first we thought she was watching the seals, but now we think not. She is communing with nature, just as we do. The difference is that she takes a leisurely time to sit, enjoy, be where she is, here, alive in the moment. She reminds me of an Indian bicycle rickshaw-walla, a man I once knew who could read and tell us interesting things about his town. After dropping me off, he would wait patiently, like so many others in India, for hours, doing nothing one could see or hear. Tuning in, perhaps. A brown study. At the time, I wondered why he didn't take a book along. I'm sure it never occurred to him. In Taiwan, I gave the designated coin to a man happily sitting by the remote roadside outside a toilet of sorts; his calling was to sell infrequent passersby two small pieces of paper. He appeared to be perfectly content with himself or the trees around him or the hot sky. These men did not need to be constantly "doing"; they were happy "being".

Anything we may read into Sharma's rapt, unmoving interest in the sea and sky in front of her appears to be far-fetched, but talk to people who have made close friends with animals and they will remark on the same thing. In an outdated, out-of-print book, *Kinship with All Life*, Allen Boone, in support of his thesis that there is no separating barrier between mineral and vegetable, between vegetable and animal, animal and man, writes of Strongheart, once a canine film "star": "To my amazement, Strongheart was not watching anything *below* him at all. His gaze was focused on a point in the sky considerably above the horizon line. He was staring off into fathomless space. Out there beyond the ability of my human senses to identify what it was, *something* was holding [his] attention."

Boone claims that just as dogs may read our minds, with patience we may learn to read theirs. In support, he mentions (rather vaguely) information he gleaned from Strongheart and recounts thoughtful and amusing episodes in his life with the German shepherd. Like the quantum physicists, and knowing nothing of their theories, he wipes out distance in communication; once established the relationship is there:

> I did not have to be within range of Strongheart's physical observation for him correctly to read my thinking and know all about my plans. He could do it across distances as easily as though he were sitting at my side. For instance, once or twice each week I would have luncheon at a Los Angeles club that was over a dozen miles away from where Strongheart and I lived. Whenever I did this a friend would stay at the house and keep an eye on the dog. There was never any set time for my returning, but at the precise moment when I decided to leave the club and come home Strongheart would always quit whatever he happened to be doing, take himself to his favourite spot for observation, and patiently wait there for me to turn the bend in the road and head up the hill.

Boone admires his dog for living abundantly in the now, without the restrictions imposed by time and space, and points out animals' ability, which we have apparently lost, to read the whole person, to know the other. He claims to have verified this through his communication with the dog:

> Strongheart . . . knew that each of [our
> visitors] was constantly broadcasting the real
> facts about himself, his thinking, his feelings
> and his emotions. Nothing that any of them
> did on the outside could possibly hide these
> facts from the dog or from any other alert ani-
> mal. . . .
>
> No matter where I happened to be or what
> I am doing my mind is always much more on
> display than my physical body and the clothes
> I happen to be wearing. Neither my inner life
> nor his inner life nor the inner life of any other
> living thing is private or concealable. We are
> all mental nudists. . . .

Quantum physicists, mystics, and some animal observ-
ers appear to agree that we, and all we feel and see, form part
of a whole; nothing is separate once a connection has been
established. Nothing is lost. We are not alone on a lonely planet.

Deep in our histories, we know this. In myth, legend,
and fairy tale, birds, insects, fish, and animals arrive at the right
moment to teach and help the suffering or confused
protagonists. A horse flies, aiding the hero; a frog goes through
a transformation in expediting the developing humanity of a
narcissistic princess; insects help Psyche outwit jealous
Aphrodite, unwilling to share her son's love; bears assume
various roles—as progenitors, princes under wicked spells,

magic helpers—in a variety of cultures.

Psychologists tell us talking animals represent our instinctual responses, are the wiser parts of ourselves. That suggests, of course, we give them this role, but possibly in some ancient reptilian area of knowing, the one in which they intuit an earthquake is about to erupt, they do have a knowledge we don't possess or don't acknowledge. On a more mundane level, it's possible they feel delicate warning tremors underfoot, but this does not account for birds' frenzied reactions to such upheavals. What world do all these forms of life inhabit? D. H. Lawrence despises his careful human education in its destruction of the numinous when it tells him always to beware and programs him to throw a log at a poisonous snake making its way back into the subterranean world after slaking its thirst at a water trough:

> And immediately I regretted it.
> I thought how paltry, how vulgar, what a mean act!
> I despised myself and the voices of my accursed human
>   education.
>
> And I thought of the albatross,
> And I wished he would come back, my snake.
>
> For he seemed to me again like a king,
> Like a king in exile, uncrowned in the underworld,
> Now due to be crowned again.
>
> And so, I missed my chance with one of the lords
> Of life.
> And I have something to expiate;
> A pettiness.

People who have endured stress, heartache, illness are learning to swim with dolphins so they may enter a peaceful realm which, for one reason or another, has been denied them. As a form of therapy, animals are now taken to visit the old and sick, those who are imprisoned away from the earth in strait rooms and nursing homes. Blind and disabled children, absorbing strength and love through legs and hands, ride horses led by volunteers.

❧

Despite all we are learning about the intimate connections between everything that exists and how little we ultimately understand the mystery of the whole, our "separate but not equal worldview is killing the planet and us along with it."[8] We still regard creatures other than ourselves as objects for our use. We are destroying ourselves in wiping out species, whether animal or plant, and we justify inflicting agony on other forms of life if we think doing so will "help mankind" or make money. I once taught with a woman who had, years before, searched for her boyfriend, a medical student, at the University of British Columbia. She walked into a secret laboratory and saw a double row of living monkeys with their brains attached to wires. The tops of their heads had been sliced off. That is no worse, of course, than chaining them, scalp removed, to specially designated tables in China where wealthy families may enjoy a gourmet meal by picking out delectable fragments of living brain with their chopsticks until the animal collapses. And perhaps it is not much worse than keeping, in Canada, large numbers of pregnant mares in "factories" to produce premarin for our hormonal needs and tonics for our hair, their foals sold, activists claim, for pet food. Some time ago, the *Sunday Observer* pictured a Japanese laboratory in which ill-tended basset hounds attempted to crawl with useless legs, fractured in tests to find a rapid cure for broken bones.

If what PETA (People for the Ethical Treatment of Animals) claims is true, it appears that those responsible for mass breeding of food in animal factories become incensed (perhaps they hate themselves?), hardly surprising considering how unpleasant but lucrative (pork is a billion dollar industry) their work must be:

> One day, the farm manager decided to kill a lame sow. After he and another employee dragged the crippled pig out of the shed, the manager took a 15-pound pipe wrench and smashed it against her head five times. The pig screamed in pain. The manager took a tiny razor blade, less than an inch long, and began to slice at her throat, at least 25 times, saying, "F—ing pig b—ch!"

We've all heard of the horrors of "downed" cows dragged to death behind trucks, of rabbits blinded by having cleaning acids tested on their eyes, of the appalling existence of battery chickens. The skull and crossbones symbol common on products informs us that we should beware: the contents have been effective enough to kill (certainly without anaesthetic) the animals on which they have been tested.

Through custom, we learn to accept that the larger the

human population grows and the more money becomes the index by which all is judged, the more animals will suffer and the more we will deplete the earth from which every single thing we use comes: all forms of energy, all food and shoes and clothes and stone and metal and earth and wood and oil and gas and vinyl and plastics. We are gobblers. We also appear to be growing pessimistic. More and more individuals are talking about another few years, after which, for one reason or another, it will all be gone. Reagan's wretched American Secretary of the Interior, born-again Christian James Watt, with hegemony over parks and the environment, started legislating the commercial use of protected natural resources since in any case the world, according to the scriptures, is about to end at any moment.

Perhaps in the final analysis our greed and stupidity does not matter. The cosmos is evolving, we are an infinitesimal part of it, nothing is finally lost. Nevertheless, it is disheartening to consider our exquisite planet and all it contains may become a failed experiment.

Hopefully, the earth is too wise to permit self-destruction and has her own way of dealing with greed and overpopulation. We trust she will not have to resort to wiping us out with painful diseases for which there are, as yet, no cure, although there are microbiologists pointing in that direction. Population in the developed world is lessening drastically with the advent of the birth control pill, the sperm count drop, and the recognition of a third sex. Developing countries will not be far behind us.

In addition to these factors, there is something else: a grassroots groundswell of caring for our earth, based perhaps on instinctive knowledge that we are a part of and connected to the whole, or perhaps simply on a natural hunger for water, shade, grass, brilliant vines, roses, extraordinary animals, sea creatures. One way we recognize our change of heart is in the legal protection of those species which were once feared and killed or which are endangered through man's predatory greed. For many of them, our eyes may be opened too late to the childish stupidity of their slaughter for prestige or for the profit which leads to despoliation of their environment.

If we could take the whole tapestry passionately into our arms, wouldn't we do so? Tree huggers literally took fragments of the whole into their arms and still do. The first were dirt poor East Indian farmers whose land was turning into desert because of deforestation; they put their bodies on the line in hugging their trees. Environmentalists across the earth have learned from them. In British Columbia, where great forests are being demolished by economic forces through multinational companies, 859 people were arrested in 1993 for civil disobedience in their attempt to halt the clear-cutting:

> On Tuesday morning, September 14, at about five a.m., standing on a logging road near the Kennedy Lake bridge, waiting to set up a living barricade against logging trucks, many people must have experienced [a] sense of awe, of quietness, of being with others and also of being alone under a vast sky filled with stars stretching, in one area, down to the horizon, stars as we never see them near city lights: enormous, pulsating constellations— giant dipper, Cassiopeia, the three brilliants

making up Orion's dagger—and single stars, planets, particularly one, growing brighter as others faded, over the peak of low mountains emerging into day. That must have been the morning star, Venus, and there she hung, surrounded by a penumbra of light while the bright silver-thin bow of the new moon rose close beside her, to her right.

As the light grew imperceptibly, the weather grew colder. Only those who kept this vigil morning after morning had brought warm enough clothes. The rest of us shivered and stuck our hands up our sleeves, but nothing would have dragged us away. Spokespeople told us the rules governing passive resistance, told us what to do when police and trucks arrived, never coerced us to risk arrest. We sang songs and some people held placards. A middle-aged man, bemused, said, "I feel as if I'm in a movie." And certainly that's what it felt like: unreal. In ghostly light, three or four hundred orderly people, a few children, all silent when they weren't singing, tired after a long, sleepless night, waited for something to happen. . . .

The police, when they arrived, were polite and pleasant. After the injunction was read . . . most of us stepped off the road. Those who remained were taken away as criminals. The loggers . . . drove by with their equipment,

Rona Murray

their eyes fixed straight ahead of them. Two mammoth boom trailers attached to self-loading trucks passed; they would carry out the corpses. But it was the stars that defied description; unsullied, ecstatically beautiful—and beyond reach.[9]

Young (and not so young) men and women are mounting nests dangerously high in trees so that, trusting to public opinion, their perches may not be demolished; they are scouring the seas for whale hunters, oil spills, and other man-made disasters; they are freeing test animals and working to save endangered species. In addition, endless books (like this one, alas), television programs, and magazine articles are appearing as advocates for the natural world.

But how can this love not find expression when, sitting here before a word processor in front of my window, wishing this book were finished so I could go wandering outside to find new and unexpected connections, I am startled by a hawk flying within a few feet, chasing (it must be admitted hawks are not vegetarians) a very small bird. Yesterday when I used a hose to water the garden, two glittering hummingbirds sprinted into the arc of streaming light and danced a cooling dance not two feet from my hand.

Evidence now supports the vision of the poet and the philosopher that plants are living, breathing, communicating creatures, endowed with personality and the attributes of soul. It is only we, in our blindness, who have insisted on considering them autonoma. Most extraordinary, it now appears that plants may be ready, willing, and able to cooperate with humanity in the Herculean job of turning this planet back into a garden from the squalor and corruption of what England's pioneer ecologist William Cobbett would have called a 'wen'.

This quotation is the final paragraph in the introduction by Peter Tompkins and Christopher Bird to their book *The Secret Life of Plants*. When this account first appeared in 1973 it caused a considerable stir but after fierce attacks discrediting it by scientists who had attempted without success to replicate experiments the authors cited, it has pretty well disappeared. In 1992, Paul Simons, a biologist, television producer, and writer, in *The Action Plant* apparently dismisses *The Secret Life* as "a clear-cut snub to the orthodox scientific community, who were outraged when the reputable journal *Science* appeared to lend some credibility by publishing a review, albeit critical." Later, however, he goes on to temper his own criticism by examining plants such as the Venus flytrap and mimosa, both of which produce touch-sensitive electrical signals—signals that exhibit distinct similarities to those which lead to the contraction of muscle cells in animals.

Simons concludes that the idea of plants having a sense of touch (of an innate sensitivity) is no longer considered outlandish and "growing evidence suggests that the nervous systems of plants and animals have more in common than was once thought." And again: "But most of all, the similarities between plants and animals are astonishing. For a botanist like myself, brought up to believe that plants are somewhat apathetic organisms, this is a revelation. Their range of sensitivity is sometimes comparable with or even surpasses that of animals. . . . They can behave in the same way: receptor potentials, action potentials, memory systems and habituation learning. They even have hormones like insulin, prostaglandins and oestrogens. And so the list goes on." He points out, "It's a remarkable coincidence that salicylic acid (the active ingredient of aspirin) blocks both the plant and animal responses to injury" and that "this latest research also point[s] to signs of communication between plants."

In at least some respects the more contemporary botanist, Simons, appears to be supporting claims by Tompkins and Bird, who suggest plant life communicates within its own form and beyond by using electrical currents. The chief criticism of the original work—Tompkins is a writer, Bird a biologist—is that the countless experiments to which they refer in order to substantiate their view that plants are sensitive to other forms of life cannot be verified under scientifically controlled conditions. Galston and Slayman in "The Not-So-Secret Life of Plants" (1979) are damning: "Quoting from uncontrolled experiments, random observations, and anecdotal reports, the book fashioned a case for the ability of plants to count, to communicate with each other, and to receive signals from life forms elsewhere in the universe. Plants were said to respond favourably to certain forms of music . . . and even to transmute elements (in order to avoid mineral starvation)."[10]

Knowing nothing but hoping for everything, a simple observer like me—scientifically uneducated, remembering D. H. Lawrence and his "accursed human education" which negates the numinous—enjoys outlandish possibilities: possibilities that may at some time be re-examined if only because we live in an extraordinary world which often appears to be not what is, for the moment and from our point of view, verifiable. We can look back at "plants were said even to transmute elements (in order to avoid mineral starvation)" and recall the recent scientific excitement over the lowly scented geranium and its enthusiasm for cleaning up waste dumps with their toxic chemicals.

Similarly, we can look again at the comments on plants responding to music. Simons opens a chapter with a far-fetched anecdote:

> Solomon Islanders can reputedly kill trees by creeping up on them at dawn and suddenly uttering piercing yells close to the trunk. The tree is supposed to die a month later. Perhaps that seems incredible, but "ordinary" plants are surprisingly sensitive to touch. . . . Indeed plants are so sensitive to mechanical sensation that Canadian biologists were able to improve growth by means of strong sound vibrations . . . perhaps giving some credibility to the Solomon Islanders' feats.

This comment returns us to one of my favourite, because

of its humour, experiments cited by Tompkins and Bird: sets of plants were isolated in containers and tested to find out how they responded to varieties of music ("sound vibrations") after it was proved they grew faster and sturdier when listening to tuneful recordings, just as cows give more milk when their barns are melodious. One container held an activated tape of modern rock and the plants' reaction was to stretch away as far as possible from the source of the sound; the other container held a tape playing classical music and the plants grew towards it so enthusiastically they entwined themselves into the player. If plants feel abused by acid rock, what effect is popular modern music having on us? It's hard to take this seriously, but the experimenters are serious. I've also heard (unverified) that similar tests have been done with pop and classical music on humans— tribal peoples and university students—with similar results.

Tompkins and Bird also consider favourably the conclusions of Davidovich Kirlian, the Russian electrician and amateur photographer, who, with his wife Valtina, produced photographs which they claimed exposed the auras of, and light streams emanating from, plants. Their universe corresponds with that of Andy Lakey after his recovery from near death due to a drug overdose. The Russians photographed a hidden world of electrical energies, publicized in the 1950s:

> Leaves from plants . . . revealed a phantasma-
> goria hitherto restricted to clairvoyants, a
> micro-universe of tiny starry points of light.
> White, blue, and even red and yellow flares
> were pictured surging out of what seemed to
> be channels in the leaves. These emanations,

or force fields round a leaf, became distorted if the leaf was mutilated, gradually diminishing and disappearing as the leaf was allowed to die. The Kirlians were next able to magnify this luminescence by adapting their photographic processes to optical instruments and microscopes. Rays of energy and whirling fireballs of light appeared to shoot out of plants into space. (Tompkins and Bird)

The authors refer to Dr. John Pierrakos, a psychiatrist, who perceived auras around plants, animals, and people, and who described all living matter as imbued with forces which "throb and pulsate like the beat of a heart." The pulsations, forming an energy field, expand and contract, grow and diminish, depending on the well-being of the plant or animal. Interested in the communication between plants and humans, Pierrakos experimented with chrysanthemums, finding that, placed beside a disturbed (screaming) patient, their lower leaves started drooping and within three days the plants were dead. On the other hand, flowers and vegetables greeted with love and admiration (not necessarily spoken; vegetation responded telepathically, like Boone's animals) thrived. They apparently acknowledged each other's pain or death and their own wounding (even a perpetrator's *intent* to wound), as well as the stress (anger, pain, violence) generated by people, but wisely "fainted" before being killed themselves.

Similar to quantum physicists, Tompkins and Bird arrived at the conclusion that the cosmos consists of electromagnetic energy with its particles forming the essential fabric of plant and animal life and generating the indivisible unity between all matter, animate and inanimate. The chrysanthemums, like other plants they specify, "picked up" on the vibrations of the psychiatric patient since they were connected through electric pulses with her fear or pain. The authors discuss plant reactions as affected by, not only their surrounding loops of calm or dislocation and varieties of music, but also by radiation from earth metals like iron and tin.

Throwing caution to the wind, they accept the existence of a whole stratum of entities such as devas and nature spirits who work with the vegetative world. In their enthusiasm, and looking for proof of these sublime "workers", they describe the exceptional gardens at Findhorn, a barren, rocky area in Scotland with a wretched climate, as an example of the harmonious and unified world we have trouble comprehending: an understandable conundrum since Findhorn's devas exist, if they do, outside the range of our senses. I have to admit I have more faith in compost, seaweed, and good manure but would madly enjoy being proved wrong, as I may be, having spoken to a recent visitor to Findhorn who said the gardens are still miraculous despite their desolate environment.

For me the most fascinating aspect of the groundswell in the enthusiastic love for our planet, daily more fervent, is that so many of us are crazy about gardening. In North America this is the number one recreational activity, noted as engaging more minds and moneys than all sports and cultural activities.

We are literally on our knees. We rush to plant sales. We

agonize over what to do with aphids and slugs and snails: all things considered, can we kill them with impunity when they must have their own useful roles? We are becoming Jains. Soon we will be forced to sweep our garden paths as we walk along them to avoid killing incarnations of our grandmothers; we will have to take to wearing masks so we don't inadvertently breathe in small creatures. In the meantime, we bury our grateful faces in apricot-yellow roses.

Garden nurseries, journals, lecturers, TV programs (I appeared in one with an excellent title, "Guerrilla Gardeners"; yes, we steal seeds and cuttings) are sprouting up like mushrooms.

On the whole, we are not competitive; on the whole, it is not to keep up with our neighbours that we spend hours weeding, watering, planting, scouting out manure and seaweed, dreaming of the dark friable earth into which we hope to turn our compost. Most gardeners spend their time in this pursuit because they love it, and perhaps plants actually do respond to that admiration and passion. Tompkins and Bird suggest they are hurt by human put-downs and glow less enthusiastically, even dwindle away, if compared unfavourably with a sister or cousin. We attempt to avoid comparisons, but it is difficult.

Interestingly enough, in a time when penurious young women will buy hyacinths to feed the soul rather than hoarding bread to feed the body, concurring with the Arabic verse—"If of thy slender store/ Thou hast but two loaves left,/ Sell one, and with the dole/ Buy hyacinths to feed Thy soul"—the largest plant wholesale business on our large island has just gone bankrupt. I've been informed by a knowledgeable gardener that the man who owned it claimed one could tell the success of

Rona Murray

such an enterprise by looking at the burn pile: the larger, the better. Anything that didn't sell rapidly should be demolished. Now he is demolished.

When a businessman with these ideas appears on the horizon, I like to think of Van Gogh and a tribute paid to him in 1891 by Octave Mirbeau, French art critic and ultimate buyer of that exquisite painting, *Irises*:

> Even in the abandonment of fantastic flowers, which rear up and ruffle their feathers like demented birds, van Gogh invariably maintained his admirable qualities as a painter, a moving mobility and a tragic grandeur which is terrifying. . . . Oh, how he understood the exquisite soul of flowers.

The authors of *The Secret Life* produced a book packed with detail on the alleged sensitivity of plants in their reaction to love, admiration, caring, but they made no attempt to account for hidden wildflowers and desert bloomers which are obviously on their own. Of course, if you go all the way with quantum physicists, they are not there, in any case, until you see them. The New Scientists appear (to one who has merely read accounts of their opinions), to be returning to the cosmology of George Berkeley, eighteenth-century eccentric Irish Anglican bishop and philosopher. His celebrated theory stipulated "to be is to be perceived"; and further that the material world is a world of ideas which only exist when they are encountered (projected?) by the mind.

However, we live in what appears to be the real world, and we dismiss what cannot be perceived by the senses even when told as children at school that nothing is solid, that the table on which we may wickedly carve a name is a mass of moving molecules. Personally, I love to run my hand along a well-crafted table. But I am also drawn toward the possibility of a dancing atomic oneness, of a cosmos united by limitless connections, the map of a spider's web; of time and space, distance, past and present merely constructs to do, for one reason or another, God knows why, with the infinitesimal life we live on earth.

If I can think this way for only a moment, I begin to return, briefly, to the timeless consciousness I knew when my car was demolished while making its way through a gravel pit one bless edly sunny January day: a day so enchanting after a grey winter, I was dreaming of turning the sod in a rain-wet garden.

$\mathcal{W}$HOLE CLOTH

※

SOME PEOPLE WHO HAVE HAD THE EXPERIENCE I've been discussing apparently change their lives dramatically, a few slightly, others not at all. Of course, the interesting question is why the discrepancy, and how does one live afterwards, no matter what generated the unexpected swoosh of ecstasy. Since my own fortunate encounter occurred during a car accident, and most of the damage to my body has been repaired, I shall remain with that.

Many people who survive bad accidents are physically and psychologically damaged far more than I was and have had to come to terms with the consequences. Some of them may have had a similar revelation; some may not. There are those, often young people, who swim into the water life has offered them without bitterness. They are survivors of remarkable resilience. But apart from the physical and psychological results, there are for some, the spiritual promptings, possibilities, beckonings. How does one respond to them? Is there any real change after this unexpected, shatteringly beautiful experience? How does the body recover, and the brain if there has been a brain injury? Is there growth? If so, can one recognize it? The gift given is positive; the negative lies in handling results which may entail pain, limited mobility, lack of energy, awareness of aging; loss of mental agility, balance, and memory; knowledge of frailty and the swift, ephemeral quality of time. Above all, how does one make sense of life and come to terms with what is to be sought, what abandoned?

Speaking from my own experience, life largely returns to its former circles, habits, compulsions. I tidy rooms already tidy, work in the garden, review plays, sit in the hot tub, go to my desk where I don't accomplish a great deal. My brain was damaged, particularly my short-term memory, but is supposedly healing. Perhaps it is. At my age it will probably never heal completely and it has sudden confusions and temporary lapses I've learned to live with. Disconcertingly, names of people, writers, titles, plants, and often words themselves, simply evaporate. I have become dependent on my life-saving thesaurus. I'll never walk or swim with the energy and enthusiasm I once possessed, but then I'm accumulating years and I suppose, unfortunately, this is to be expected.

The years themselves are unimportant to me. Before the accident, I didn't really think about them. I just appeared to go on being the same person and age I had always been, although I obviously was not. Students and friends were generally at least a generation or more younger than I was, but that didn't make much or any difference, at least to me. It probably did to them. But thinking of all this candidly, for an active but somewhat physically unenthusiastic person like me, it's a relief not to be a jogger, a fitness addict, a shopper, a frequenter of hair stylists, in an attempt to hang on to evaporated youth. I prefer to think, like Sartre, that by the time I was twenty-five, I was responsible for the lines on my face, and I have no desire to eradicate them—to become faceless—with expensive oils and operations.

Allowing one's specific age to dictate thoughts and feelings appears absurd. Even so, I'm stunned at how fast time goes by, is shrivelled up, and how little the inside changes while the outside loses its strength, grows frail. I'm beginning to feel (against my deep-down self) curiously grateful to those individuals my children's age who are there to support me with their friendship.

On the positive side of the agenda, I can say truthfully that I am more in love with the physical earth and all it contains than I ever was before. There is an added importance in recognizing how favoured we are, how blessed, how generosity of spirit is good and how generating want and pain is evil. I used not to believe in evil. Now I do: not in any kind of pathetic devil but in a fatal flaw in ourselves, in our stunning lack of imagination, of empathy, of concern for those to whom we cause excruciating pain. So often we waste our time living ego-centred, isolated, sundered lives: "We have met the enemy, and he is us."

I heard Nobel Laureate William Golding give a reading some years ago. What I remember chiefly is that afterwards, in an off-the-cuff remark, he said with unshakable fervour: "This world is hell, but I know perfect goodness exists somewhere." If this world is hell, and certainly for many people it is, it is we who make it so. How could we find an earth more various, more inventive, more physically exquisite?

※

I should like to end this extended essay with two images.

In the summer of 1995, we recognized the end of the Second World War: VJ Day—the fiftieth anniversary. "Sunday Morning" on CBC Radio ran a program, originating in Australia, on the fire bombing of a Japanese city. The pilots of the American planes had been told the Japanese manufactured parts for war machines—planes, tanks, guns—and munitions in their houses so destruction was to be total. This was not true. Factories manufactured war implements. But perhaps it made it easier for the bombers to act without mercy. At least, so a gentle-voiced Texan—a former pilot—recounted. He was describing the destruction from the air, the fires and the stench of burning flesh. Others, children and young people at the time, described it from the ground: the bombs which exploded, shooting out tongues of white-hot material, the velocity of the winds, the small lakes into which people ran and jumped, hoping to escape the agonizing heat. They jammed into the water, row on row, like sardines in a can, and were asphyxiated, air snatched away from noses held above water. Or they boiled alive.

A couple of weeks later, we saw TV footage on what the atomic bombs accomplished. President Harry Truman announced that Hiroshima was a military target. Almost all those killed were women and children. The children were, if they were old enough, on their way to school, carrying books and lunch kits. If they weren't at once entirely incinerated, the skin ran off their bodies in bloody red strips like torn sheeting. The death toll, including those bombed in the small city of

Nagasaki and those who died later of radiation, rose to at least 200,000. On film taken at the time, terribly wounded survivors make no fuss, look stunned. And again later, surviving children turn round obediently, showing how their skin is in tatters, their hair falling out, their limbs deformed. They have small, closed, calm faces.

Our Prime Minister, Mackenzie-King, wrote in his diary, "It is fortunate that the use of the bomb should have been upon the Japanese rather than upon the white races of Europe." Physicist J. Robert Oppenheimer quoted the Bhagavad-Gita: "I am become Death, the shatterer of worlds."[11]

When travelling in Japan in the early seventies, I was in a town—Osaka or Kyoto—with a small lake. After school, children in tunics or trousers with immaculate white shirts went there to practise on classical instruments. Their music floated from one part of the lake to another, a violin answering a cello, a flute calling to an oboe. Together they were unknowingly weaving a fabric of wholeness. It was exceptionally quiet for a city, and exceptionally peaceful.

One of the Blessings in the Hebrew marriage ceremony tells us: "Blessed is the design of the human being. Developing our wisdom and compassion we may become God-like. We are assembled from the very fabric of the universe, and are composed of eternal elements."

The woven "whole cloth" in Indian traditional culture is seen as "a fabric woven by the gods. The cosmos, the ordered universe is one continuous fabric with its warp and woof making a grid pattern. The importance of wholeness is seen in the uncut garment as in the *sari* and *dhoti* and also in the cloth woven all in one piece on which a sacred painting is made. Whether as a covering for the body or as a ground for painting, the uncut fabric is a symbol of totality and integrity."[12]

If a rag is offered at a shrine to Chindt ya Deo, the Lord of Tatters, a whole cloth will be returned.

We don't need to live trivial lives. In the frantic disorder of the postmodern world, it is still possible to weave the whole cloth, to find unity in the miraculous possibilities of silence, and to listen, as this six-year-old child listened for the moon to speak to him through a simple seed and to give him knowledge we all seek:

> I planted a seed.
> It's like the moon.
>
> It's like the moon
> is speaking to me
> through the seed's hole
> and trying to teach me.[13]

> Iwagati Takuya

NOTES

1. Keene, *Anthology of Japanese Literature.*

2. Ramanujan, *Speaking of Shiva*.

3. Untermeyer, *Modern American Poetry.*

4. Presumably this suggests an overflowing of energy in every direction.

5. Guy Dauncey, "Your View," *Victoria Times Colonist,* 12 October 1999.

6. Rosemary Sullivan, review of *Private Myths* in the *Globe and Mail,* 30 March 1996.

7. *The Inferno of Dante,* Canto 1.

8. Jim Nollman, "The Secret Language of the Wild," *Utne Reader,* March–April 1998.

9. Murray, in *Witness to Wilderness.*

10. *American Scientist* 67:337.

11. Carl Mollins, "Paying for the bomb," *Macleans,* 7 August 1995.

12. Graburn, *Ethnic and Tourist Arts.*

13. Navasky, *Festival in My Heart.*

Rona Murray's Poetry Selections

p. 27 "Visitation." Unpublished.

p. 31 "It was then that I met my angel." Published in *Selected Poems*. Victoria, BC: Sono Nis Press, 1974.

p. 47 "Each one." Published in *Journey*. Victoria, BC: Sono Nis Press, 1981.

p. 52 "The Dark." Published in *Selected Poems*.

p. 60 "Hives, aromatic with propolis . . ." Excerpt from *The Lost Garden* (chapbook). Victoria, BC: Hawthorne Society/ Reference West, 1993.

p. 75 Poem for Brent. Untitled, unpublished.

p. 87 "I celebrate." Published in *Selected Poems*.

p. 91 "Homing." Published in *Journey*.

p. 102 "July ends . . ." Untitled, unpublished.

p. 105 "Blackberries." Published in *Journey*.

p. 115 "The Hunter." Published in *Selected Poems*.

BIBLIOGRAPHY

Bettelheim, Bruno. *The Uses of Enchantment: The Meaning and Importance of Fairy Tales.* New York: Vintage, 1954.

Boone, J. Allen. *Kinship with All Life.* New York: Harper & Brothers, 1954.

Bucke, Richard Maurice. *Cosmic Consciousness: A Study in the Evolution of the Human Mind.* New York: E. P. Dutton, 1954.

Dante, Alighieri. *The Inferno of Dante,* Robert Pinsky, trans. New York: Farrar, Straus & Giroux, 1994.

Davies, Paul, and John Gribbin. *The Matter Myth: Dramatic Discoveries That Challenge Our Understanding of Physical Reality.* New York: Simon & Schuster, 1992.

Ferguson, John, ed. *An Illustrated Encyclopedia of Mysticism and the Mystery Religions.* New York: Seabury Press, 1977.

Ghiselin, Brewster, ed. *The Creative Process: A Symposium.* New York: New American Library, 1961

Graburn, Nelson H. H. *Ethnic and Tourist Arts: Cultural Expressions from the Fourth World.* Berkeley: University of California Press, 1976.

Grimble, Arthur. *A Pattern of Islands.* London: John Murray, 1952.

Hopkins, Gerard Manley. *Poems of Gerard Manley Hopkins.* New York: Oxford University Press, 1948.

Hove, Philo H. 1999. *Wonder and the Agencies of Retreat.* Unpublished doctoral dissertation, University of Alberta.

John of the Cross, St. *Dark Night of the Soul: A Classic in the Literature of Mysticism by St. John of the Cross,* Edgar Allison Peers, trans. and ed. New York: Image Books, 1962.

Jung, Carl G. *Memories, Dreams, Reflections.* Recorded and edited by Aniela Jaffé. New York: Vintage, 1963.

Jung, Carl G., with Marie-Luise von Franz. *Man and His Symbols.* London: Doubleday, 1964.

Keene, Donald, ed. *Anthology of Japanese Literature: From the Earliest Era to the Mid-Nineteenth Century.* New York: Grove Press, 1955.

Lawrence, D. H. *Selected Poems.* New York: Viking Press, 1967.

Lakey, Andy. *Art, Angels, and Miracles.* Atlanta: Turner Publishing, 1996.

Lowry, Malcolm. *Hear Us O Lord from Heaven Thy Dwelling Place.* New York: J.B. Lippincott, 1961.

Mann, Thomas. "Dostoevsky in Moderation." Introduction to *The Short Novels of Dostoevsky,* Constance Garnett, trans. New York: Dial Press, 1945.

Murray, Rona. "Waiting by the Bridge." In *Witness to Wilderness: The Clayoquot Sound Anthology,* Howard Breen-Needham *et al.,* eds. Vancouver: Arsenal Pulp Press, 1994.

Navasky, Bruno, trans. and ed. *Festival in My Heart: Poems by Japanese Children.* New York: Harry N. Abrams, 1993.

Ramanujan, A. K., trans. *Speaking of Shiva*. Middlesex: Penguin, 1985.

Raymo, Chet. *The Soul of the Night: An Astronomical Pilgrimage*. New Jersey: Prentice Hall, 1985.

Rensberger, Boyce. *Instant Biology: From Single Cells to Human Beings and Beyond*. New York: Fawcett Columbine, 1996.

Rilke, Rainer Maria. *The Selected Poetry of Rainer Maria Rilke*, Stephen Mitchell, trans. and ed. New York: Vintage, 1989.

Rumi, Jalal al-Din. *The Essential Rumi*, Coleman Barks, trans. New York: HarperCollins, 1995.

Simons, Paul. *The Action Plant: Movement and Nervous Behaviour in Plants*. Oxford: Blackwell, 1992.

Thomas, Lewis. *The Lives of a Cell: Notes of a Biology Watcher*. Toronto: Bantam, 1975.

Tompkins, Peter, and Christopher Bird. *The Secret Life of Plants*. London: Allen Lane, 1974.

Underhill, Evelyn. *Mysticism: A Study in the Nature and Development of Man's Spiritual Consciousness*. New York: Meridian, 1955.

Untermeyer, Louis. *Modern American Poetry, Modern British Poetry*. New York: Harcourt, Brace & Co., 1919.

Walker, Kenneth. *Diagnosis of Man*, 2nd ed. London: Jonathan Cape, 1943.

Wheatley, Margaret J. *Leadership and the New Science: Learning about Organization from an Orderly Universe*. San Francisco: Berrett-Koehler, 1992.

Whitman, Walt. *Leaves of Grass*. New York: New American Library, 1958.

Wilder, Thornton. *The Bridge of San Luis Rey*. New York: Albert and Charles Boni, 1927.

Young, Patricia. *What I Remember from My Time on Earth: Poems*. Toronto: House of Anansi, 1997.

Zukav, Gary. *The Dancing Wu Li Masters: An Overview of the New Physics*. New York: Quill, 1979.

Journey

"A sensitive, moving and skilful poet."—*Canadian Literature*

"A poet of great energy, taut phrasing, and a keening lyricism." —*THE AMERICAN POETRY REVIEW*

ISBN 0-919462-75-8 • $8.95

Journey Back to Peshawar

Journey Back to Peshawar vividly recalls Murray's early years in the India of the British Raj and her return 50 years later to the very different India of the 1980s. Beautifully written, this is a riveting story of India then and now.

"The way *Journey Back to Peshawar* slides between family tradition and personal experience sets a perfect tone."
—STEPHEN INGLIS, CANADIAN MUSEUM OF CIVILIZATION

"Murray's is the sort of book most writers dream of writing. Certainly it is the book we all dream of reading."
—CHARLES LILLARD

ISBN 1-55039-034-1 • $14.95

Selected Poems

"The erect stone on the skyline shores up more than what it touches. It will fasten like a splint to the fractured eye and the eye will consume it, and the stone will continue to stand. Rona Murray's poems have that abiding uprightness. They leave their permanent registration on the retina of the language and on—to use her words—the retina of the heart."

—ROBERT BRINGHURST

ISBN 0-919462-11-1 • $8.95 (cloth)

Threshold: Six Women, Six Poets
(edited by Rona Murray)

Rona Murray presents the poems of six vibrant female poets, each on the threshold of her professional literary career: Alisa Gordaneer, Dorothy Field, Suzanne Steele, Susan Stenson, Kelly Parsons, and Barbara Colebrook Peace.

"These poems come to us beautifully realized. This is the work of women who have been observing, ruminating, and practising their craft for some time, perhaps in private, perhaps sharing with only a few friends. Rona Murray has done us a great favour gathering their voices together. As I was reading this book, I sensed each poet passing over the 'threshold' into our communal, poetic landscape, each one speaking her own rhythms, speaking passionately what she knows."

—PATRICIA YOUNG

ISBN 1-55039-092-9 • $14.95

Rona Murray was born in London, England, in 1924. She spent her early childhood in India and immigrated to Canada in 1932. Since then, she has travelled the world extensively. She has a Ph.D. in English Literature from the University of Kent at Canterbury, England, and has spent over twenty-five years teaching English and Creative Writing in universities throughout British Columbia. Dr. Murray is an award-winning author/editor of thirteen books. Widely known as one of Canada's most treasured poets, she has also received accolades for her short stories, creative non-fiction, and memoirs. She has written four plays, which have been produced in Canada and the United States. Dr. Murray and her husband, potter Walter Dexter, currently reside on Vancouver Island.